Unsolved
MIRACLES

Unsolved
MIRACLES

compiled by *John Van Diest*

Multnomah Publishers Sisters, Oregon

UNSOLVED MIRACLES
published by Multnomah Publishers, Inc.

© 1997 by Multnomah Publishers, Inc.
International Standard Book Number: 1-57673-226-6

Cover photo Adobe Image Library
Printed in the United States of America

For information:
MULTNOMAH PUBLISHERS, INC.
POST OFFICE BOX 1720
SISTERS, OREGON 97759

Library of Congress Cataloging-in-Publication Data:
Unsolved miracles/compiled by John Van Diest.   p.cm.   ISBN 1-57673-150-2
1. Miracles. 2. Angels. 3. Healing--Religious aspects. 4. Religious biography.
I. Van Diest, John. BT97.2.U57   1997   97-19581 CIP   231.7'3–dc21

99 00 01 02 03 04 05 — 10 9 8 7 6 5 4 3 2

To my mother, Tress, who lives in Portland

surrounded by her children,

grandchildren, and great-grandchildren.

To my father, John Sr., who lives in heaven

surrounded by angels.

To my wife, Pat, who lives with me and

has surrounded me with more than

forty years of companionship,

love, and encouragement.

APPRECIATION

To the many authors, whose stories are this book: a sincere debt of gratitude—it's really your book.

To Don and Vera Hillis, for your willingness to include miracle stories from your collection—thank you.

To Linda Rogers, whose testimony planted the seed for this book.

To Alice Gray, Casandra Lindell, and Shari MacDonald, whose combined skills "made it happen."

Contents

Preface   13

MIRACLES OF DESTINY   17

It Happened on a Brooklyn Subway *by Paul Deutschman*
The Bullet *by Doris Sanford*
The Gold and Ivory Tablecloth *by Howard C. Schade*
Divine Honeymoon *by James Dobson*
Rescue Fire *by Billy Graham*
Strange Angels *by Jan Winebrenner*
The Men with the Bibles
Miracle in the Details *by Jerry Jenkins*

MIRACLES OF PROVISION   45

Guiding Signs *by Dawn Raffel*
A Small Girl's Prayer *by Helen Roseveare*
Tornado! *by Joan Wester Anderson*
When the Rain Came *by Una Roberts Lawrence*
Mary's Secret List *by Barb Marshall*
Providence Spring *by J.C. Sills*
The Bridge That Wasn't There *by Howard Foltz*
An Unlikely Rain *by Doris Sanford*
Faith and Action *by Henry T. Blackaby and Claude V. King*
My Encourager *by Kenneth Taylor*
The Music Box *by Sherry Angel*
One Thousand Dollars Short *by Bernie May*
Right on Top *by Mother Teresa*

MIRACLES AND ANGELS   81

In A Moment of Time *by Hope MacDonald*
Safely Home *by Joan Wester Anderson*
Marching Orders *by Corri ten Boom*
On A Winter Night *by Billy Graham*
Intervention on the Front Lines *by David Jeremiah*
Missed Overalls *by Sam Graham Humphreys*
Large Fiery Figures *by David Jeremiah*
A Voice of Warning *by Hope MacDonald*
Through Gates of Splendor *by Olive Fleming Liefeld*
Stranger at the Gate *by V. Raymond Edman*
As Tall as Trees *by Marilynn Carlson Webber and
William D. Webber*
A Prisoner…and Yet *by Corrie ten Boom*
Two Came for Katherine retold *by Gary Kinnaman*

MIRACLES FOR EVERYDAY LIFE   115

Incredible *by David Jeremiah*
A Shield of Protection *by Pat Robertson*
Don't *Ever* Let Your Guard Down *by Donald Jacobson*
Please Lord, Let Her Live *by Kenneth Taylor*
Stop the Rain, Lord *by Adrian Rogers*
An Unseen Hand to Guide the Course *by Sara Boyd*
A Dive of Faith *by James Dobson*
A Dead End *by Ron Mehl*
Great Balls of Fire *by Rodney Charles*

MIRACLES OF PRAYER   151

Selling Cattle *by Howard Hendricks*
Covered with a Cloud *by Spencer January*
Angry Guard Dogs *by Robert P. Dugan, Jr.*
I Put "New Car" on My Prayer List *by Linda Rogers*

Twenty-seven Soldiers *by Billy Graham*
Danger in the Canyon *by Andrea Gross*
The Silent Alarm *by Doris Sanford*

MIRACLES OF HEALING 171

A Hand on Her Shoulder *by Andrea Gross*
Beautiful Eyes *by Adrian Rogers*
Getting Straightened Out *by Tony Campolo*
Our Daughter's Cancer *by Henry T. Blackaby*
Buried Alive! *by Beth Mullally*
Miracle in My Family *by Dale Hanson Bourke*
The House Church in China *by Carl Lawrence*

MIRACLES OF CHANGED LIVES 203

We Were inRow Twenty-Six *by John Aker*
Jesus…and Jim *by J. Sidlow Baxter*
Project Pearl *by Jeff Taylor*
Uncle Roger *by Rebecca Manley Pippert*
Let's Sing It! *by Charles Colson*
A Place of Peace *by Jeff Taylor*

THE TWO GREATEST MIRACLES 229

God Came *by Joni Eareckson Tada*
Extraordinary Moment *by Max Lucado*

A FINAL WORD 239

NOTES 245

PREFACE

I don't know about you, but I've always been a bit skeptical when it comes to the subject of modern miracles. It's one thing to trust scriptural accounts of unexplained phenomena. But contemporary miraculous events? I'm a reasonable, educated man. I'm not impressed by supermarket tabloid headlines. Yes, I believe God works in mysterious ways. But such mysteries have never been a part of my everyday experience. The world I live in is rational, ordered, easily explained.

At least, I used to think so.

A couple of years ago, I pictured all miracles as dramatic, Technicolor events. If you had told me then that you had experienced a miracle, I probably would have smiled politely and scanned the room for the nearest emergency exit. I might have questioned whether you knew the definition of the word, or wondered aloud if you had ever seen Cecil B. DeMille's *The Ten Commandments*.

Now *those* were what I call miracles. A burning bush that was not consumed by fire. Wooden staffs turning to snakes. Moses parting the Red Sea. I could accept those miracles as true because they were straight out of the Bible, which I believe in quite literally.

Through years of study, I've discovered that miracles occur throughout the biblical text. Peter walking on water, Jesus healing the blind man, Lazarus being raised from the dead…it's all there in black and white. Biblical times called for biblical miracles. I can accept that. But as the saying goes: that was then, and this is now. It's a commonly held belief that God doesn't intervene in the natural order of things anymore. It isn't that he can't, he just doesn't.

Or does he?

Despite my skepticism and doubts, I have ultimately been confronted with overwhelming evidence to convince me that miracles still occur today. Not all are the sweeping, major motion picture type (although many would rival today's typical Hollywood story lines). Yet to the individuals who experienced them, these miracles are every bit as dramatic, every bit as life-changing as the emancipation of Israel.

In compiling this collection, I've sifted through hundreds of amazing stories about modern-day miracles to find the most interesting, the most compelling accounts. These include stories written by respected authors such as Billy Graham, James Dobson, Corrie ten Boom, Mother Teresa, and Adrian Rogers, as well as writers you may not yet know but whose words may forever impact what you believe about miracles.

These stories defy what most of us consider "reasonable" explanation. Yet, like me, you may soon find evidence that convinces you what is "reasonable" is not always the same as what is true. You may come to believe that a loving God is active and present and involved in our world—and that this God *is* a God of miracles.

Of course, you don't have to take my word for it. Examine the evidence for yourself. Within these pages, you'll find dramatic accounts about the occurrence of modern-day miracles. Of the hundreds of stories reviewed, the ones selected were chosen because:

1. The sources were highly credible
2. The events or circumstances were not only improbable, but there was no evident "natural" explanation for their occurrence, and
3. The uniqueness of the miracles illustrates the wide variety of examples of supernatural intervention.

The purpose of this book is not to give "miracle believers" ammunition to blow away the doubts of their friends, nor is it to *prove* to the skeptics among us that modern miracles really do occur. In compiling these accounts, I have not attempted to resolve any philosophical or theological questions regarding miracles.

What I *have* tried to do is give you something to think about. Stories to consider. Claims to ponder. It's up to you to decide what *you* believe. So go ahead. Dig in. Weigh the evidence. Open your heart. God may surprise you yet, even reach into your life to do something you never thought possible.

Greater miracles have happened.

Miracles of

DESTINY

The miracles in fact are a retelling in small letters

of the very same story which is written across the whole world

in letters too large for some of us to see.

C.S. Lewis

Miracles of
DESTINY

I t was meant to be." How many times have you used those
words to describe a wonderful coincidence that brought joy
to your life? Indeed, at times there seems to be no other
explanation for the unlikely chains of events that lead to the
blessings we receive. Destiny? *Hmm,* we think, *perhaps....* The
very word intrigues us, with its implication that certain events
in our lives were preordained by One who has our ultimate
good in mind.

There is something thrilling about the prospect of a loving
God looking out for us, bringing into our lives the people and
circumstances we need—through the natural order of life and
even through miracles. Yet there is something frightening, as
well, about this belief. For if we acknowledge that God is truly
"out there," acting on our behalf, then it naturally follows that
we must decide how we will respond to him.

This may explain why we sometimes try to convince ourselves that miraculous events are really nothing more than "cos-
mic accidents." Yet there is no such thing as a true accident.
Nothing happens outside of God's plan. Though we do not

always understand his purpose, and though we struggle through times of suffering and confusion, God remains in control...always. In fact, it is frequently the very circumstances that cause us pain that God uses to bring us our greatest joy.

In the next section, you'll read about a number of men and women whose lives truly may have been touched by God's hand.

"Happy coincidences"? Acts of love? Miracles?

You decide.

IT HAPPENED ON THE BROOKLYN SUBWAY

by Paul Deutschman

The car was crowded, and there seemed to be no chance of a seat. But as I entered, a man sitting by the door suddenly jumped up to leave, and I slipped into the empty seat.

I've been living in New York long enough not to start conversations with strangers. But, being a photographer, I have the peculiar habit of analyzing people's faces, and I was struck by the features of the passenger on my left. He was probably in his late thirties, and when he glanced up, his eyes seemed to have a hurt expression in them. He was reading a Hungarian-language newspaper, and something prompted me to say in Hungarian, "I hope you don't mind if I glance at your paper."

The man seemed surprised to be addressed in his native language. But he only answered politely, "You may read it now. I'll have time later on."

During the half-hour ride to town, we had quite a conversation. He said his name was Bela Paskin. A law student when World War II started, he had been put into a German labor battalion and sent to the Ukraine. Later he was captured by the Russians and put to work burying the German dead. After the war, he covered hundreds of miles on foot until he reached his home in Debrecen, a large city in eastern Hungary.

I myself knew Debrecen quite well, and we talked about it for a while. Then he told me the rest of his story. When he went to the apartment once occupied by his father, mother, brothers, and sisters, he found strangers living there. Then he went upstairs to the apartment that he and his wife once had. It also was occupied by strangers. None of them had ever heard of his family.

As he was leaving, full of sadness, a boy ran after him, calling, "Paskin bacsi! Paskin bacsi!" That means "Uncle Paskin." The child was the son of some old neighbors of his. He went to the boy's home and talked to his parents. "Your whole family is dead," they told him. "The Nazis took them and your wife to Auschwitz."

Auschwitz was one of the worst Nazi concentration camps. Paskin gave up all hope. A few days later, too heartsick to remain any longer in Hungary, he set out on foot again, stealing across border after border until he reached Paris. He managed to emigrate to the United States in October 1947, just three months before I met him.

All the time he had been talking, I kept thinking that somehow his story seemed familiar. A young woman whom I met recently at the home of friends had also been from Debrecen; she had been sent to Auschwitz; from there she had been transferred to work in a German munitions factory. Her relatives had been killed in the gas chambers. Later, she was liberated by the Americans and was brought here in the first boatload of displaced persons in 1946.

Her story had moved me so much that I had written down her address and phone number, intending to invite her to meet my family and thus help relieve the terrible emptiness in her life.

It seemed impossible that there could be any connection between these two people, but as I neared my station, I fumbled anxiously in my address book. I asked in what I hoped was a casual voice, "Was your wife's name Marya?"

He turned pale. "Yes!" he answered. "How did you know?"

He looked as if he were about to faint.

I said, "Let's get off the train." I took him by the arm at the next station and led him to a phone booth. He stood there like a man in a trance while I dialed her phone number.

It seemed hours before Marya Paskin answered. (Later I learned her room was alongside the telephone, but she was in the habit of never answering it because she had so few friends and the calls were always for someone else. This time, however, there was no one else at home and, after letting it ring for a while, she responded.

When I heard her voice at last, I told her who I was and asked her to describe her husband. She seemed surprised at the question, but gave me a description. Then I asked her where she had lived in Debrecen, and she told me the address.

Asking her to hold the line, I turned to Paskin and said, "Did you and your wife live on such-and-such a street?"

"Yes!" Bela exclaimed. He was white as a sheet and trembling.

"Try to be calm," I urged him. "Something miraculous is about to happen to you. Here, take this telephone and talk to your wife!"

He nodded his head in mute bewilderment, his eyes bright with tears. He took the receiver, listened a moment to his wife's voice, then suddenly cried, "This is Bela! This is Bela!" and began to mumble hysterically. Seeing that the poor fellow was so excited he couldn't talk coherently, I took the receiver from his shaking hands.

"Stay where you are," I told Marya, who also sounded hysterical. "I am sending your husband to you. We will be there in a few minutes."

Bela was crying like a baby and saying over and over again, "It is my wife. I go to my wife!"

At first I thought I had better accompany Paskin, lest the man should faint from excitement, but I decided that this was a moment in which no strangers should intrude. Putting Paskin into a taxicab, I directed the driver to take him to Marya's address, paid the fare, and said good-bye.

Bela Paskin's reunion with his wife was a moment so poignant, so electric with suddenly released emotion, that afterward neither he nor Marya could recall much about it.

"I remember only that when I left the phone, I walked to the mirror like in a dream to see if maybe my hair had turned gray," she said later. "The next thing I know, a taxi stops in front of the house, and it is my husband who comes toward me. Details I cannot remember; only this I know—that I was happy for the first time in many years...

"Even now it is difficult to believe that it happened. We have both suffered so much; I have almost lost the capability not to be afraid. Each time my husband goes from the house, I say to myself, 'Will anything happen to take him from me again?'"

Her husband is confident that no horrible misfortune will ever befall them. "Providence has brought us together," he says simply. "It was meant to be."

THE BULLET

by Doris Sanford

I t was a late March afternoon and Anya sat in the car memorizing Bible verses. She did it every week while her little brother, Zeek, had his piano lesson. Her turn would come next, but memorizing meant repeating the verses out loud and that worked best in the car. She was a part of her junior high Bible Quiz team and that required knowing a part of one of the books of the Bible *very* well. No problem. Anya loved the competition!

Their music teacher lived in a two-story house and the piano was upstairs. Just before the lesson began, Zeek told his mom, "I want Sissy to listen to my lesson." Mom reminded him that Anya needed the study time, and besides, she had been listening to him practice his piano lesson all week at home. But Zeek was determined, he went down to the car and to Mom's surprise returned with his big sister in tow.

The lesson began. Five minutes later the lesson was abruptly halted by a loud noise outside. Everyone stopped to watch a late-model car speeding away. The lesson resumed after the teacher reassured them that it was probably the car's backfire they had heard.

Zeek's hands were barely on the piano when the teacher's husband rushed in: "A gun shot...into the car...shattered the passenger side window in the front seat!" The lesson was over. They hurried down to look. Sure enough, there was the bullet lodged in the back rest just where Anya's head had been five minutes earlier.

They all knew it immediately. God had used seven-year-old Zeek to save his sister's life. It was a profound moment. Zeek had responded when it hadn't made sense to him or anyone else, and Anya had complied with his illogical request.

The two snipers who were driving through the streets of Salem, Oregon, randomly shooting at mailboxes, cars, and houses were arrested and held on one-million dollars bail. The district attorney asked Anya and Zeek to come to court and tell their story. The young men were sent to prison for five years, but not without hearing how God had protected a seven-year-old and his big sister.

Doris Sanford is the author of more than a dozen books and a teacher of psychiatric nursing.

The Gold and Ivory Tablecloth

by Howard C. Schade

Reprinted with permission from December 1954 Reader's Digest.

At Christmastime men and women everywhere gather in their churches to wonder anew at the greatest miracle the world has ever known. But the story I like best to recall was not a miracle—not exactly.

It happened to a pastor who was very young. His church was very old. Once, long ago, it had flourished. Famous men had preached from its pulpit, prayed before its altar. Rich and poor alike worshiped there and built it beautifully. Now the good days had passed from the section of town where it stood. But the pastor and his young wife believed in their run-down church. They felt that with paint, hammer, and faith they could get it in shape. Together they went to work.

But in late December a severe storm whipped through the river valley, and the worst blow fell on the little church—a huge chunk of rain-soaked plaster fell out of the inside wall just behind the altar. Sorrowfully, the pastor and his wife swept away the mess, but they couldn't hide the ragged hole.

The pastor looked at it and had to remind himself quickly, "Thy will be done!" But his wife wept, "Christmas is only two days away!"

That afternoon the dispirited couple attended the auction held for the benefit of a youth group. The auctioneer opened a box and shook out of its folds a handsome gold-and-ivory lace tablecloth. It was a magnificent item, nearly fifteen feet long. But it, too, dated from a long-vanished era. Who, today, had any use for such a thing? There were a few half-hearted bids. Then the pastor was seized with what he thought was a great idea. He bid it in for $6.50.

He carried the cloth back to the church and tacked it up on the wall behind the altar. It completely hid the hole! And the extraordinary beauty of its shimmering handwork cast a fine, holiday glow over the chancel. It was a great triumph. Happily he went back to preparing his Christmas sermon.

Just before noon on the day of Christmas Eve, as the pastor was opening the church, he noticed a woman standing in the cold at the bus stop.

"The bus won't be here for forty minutes!" he called, and invited her into the church to get warm.

She told him that she had come from the city that morning to be interviewed for a job as governess to the children of one of the wealthy families in town but she had been turned down. A war refugee, her English was imperfect.

The woman sat down in a pew and chafed her hands and rested. After a while she dropped her head and prayed. She looked up as the pastor began to adjust the great ivory-and-gold lace cloth across the hole. She rose suddenly and walked up the steps of the chancel. She looked at the tablecloth. The pastor smiled and started to tell her about the storm damage, but she didn't seem to listen. She took up a fold of the cloth and rubbed it between her fingers.

"It is mine!" she said. "It is my banquet cloth!" She lifted the corner and showed the surprised pastor that there were initials monogrammed on it. "My husband had the cloth made especially for me in Brussels! There could not be another like it."

For the next few minutes the woman and the pastor talked excitedly together. She explained that she was Viennese; that she and her husband had opposed the Nazis and decided to leave the country. They were advised to go separately. Her husband put her on a train for Switzerland. They planned that he would join her as soon as he could arrange to ship their household goods across the border.

She never saw him again. Later she heard that he had died in a concentration camp.

"I have always felt that it was my fault—to leave without him," she said. "Perhaps these years of wandering have been my punishment!"

The pastor tried to comfort her, urged her to take the cloth with her. She refused. Then she went away.

As the church began to fill on Christmas Eve, it was clear that the cloth was going to be a great success. It had been skillfully designed to look its best by candlelight.

After the service, the pastor stood in the doorway; many people told him that the church looked beautiful. One gentle-faced, middle-aged man—he was the local clock-and-watch repairman—looked rather puzzled.

"It is strange," he said in his soft accent. "Many years ago my wife—God rest her—and I owned such a cloth. In our home in Vienna, my wife put it on the table"—here he smiled—"only when the bishop came to dinner!"

The pastor suddenly became very excited. He told the jeweler about the woman who had been in the church earlier in the day.

The startled jeweler clutched the pastor's arm. "Can it be? Does she live?"

Together the two got in touch with the family who had interviewed her. Then, in the pastor's car they started for the city. And as Christmas Day was born, this man and his wife—who had been separated through so many saddened Yuletides—were reunited.

To all who heard this story, the joyful purpose of the storm that knocked a hole in the wall of the church was now quite clear. Of course, people said it was a miracle, and I think you will agree it was the season for it!

DIVINE HONEYMOON

by James Dobson

Do you believe the Lord still performs miracles today, or has the era of supernatural intervention passed? Although I am suspicious of people who attempt to market them on demand, I have no doubt that miracles still occur every day.

I can't resist sharing an incident that ranks as one of the most interesting examples of God's intervention I've ever heard. It occured in 1945, shortly after the end of World War II. A young associate pastor named Cliff and his fiancée, Billie, were anxious to get married, even though they had very little money. They managed to scrape together enough funds for a simple wedding and two train tickets to a city where he had been asked to hold a revival with a friend. By combining this responsibility with their honeymoon, they thought they could afford it. They planned to stay at a nearby resort hotel.

The couple got off the train and took a bus to the hotel, only to learn that it had been taken over by the military for use as a rehabilitation center. It was no longer open to guests. There they were, stranded in an unfamiliar city with only a few dollars between them. There was little to do but attempt to hitch a ride on the nearby highway. Soon a car pulled over, and the driver asked them where they wanted to go.

"We don't know," they said, and explained their predicament. The man was sympathetic and said perhaps he could offer a suggestion. A few miles down the road was a grocery store that was owned by a woman he knew. She had a couple of empty rooms upstairs and might be willing to let them stay there inexpensively. They were in no position to be choosy.

The woman rented them a room for $5, and they moved in. During their first day in residence, the new bride spent the afternoon practicing the piano, and Cliff played the trombone he had brought with him. The proprietor of the store sat rocking in a chair, listening to the music. When she realized they were Christians, she referred them to a friend, who invited them to spend the rest of their honeymoon in his home. Several days later, the host mentioned that a young evangelist was speaking at a youth rally at a nearby Christian conference center. They were invited to attend.

That night, it so happened that the regular song leader was sick, and Cliff was asked to take charge of the music. What a historic occasion it was! The evangelist turned out to be a very young Billy Graham. The groom was Cliff Barrows. They met that evening, and a lifetime partnership was formed. Cliff and his wife, Billie, have been members of the Billy Graham Evangelistic Association ever since that evening and were used by the Lord in thousands of crusades all around the world. I suppose Paul Harvey would say, "And now you know…the rest of the story."

James Dobson is the founder and president of Focus on the Family Ministries, and author of numerous best-selling books including When God Doesn't Make Sense.

RESCUE FIRE

by Billy Graham

A lone survivor of a shipwreck was marooned on an uninhabited island. He managed to build a hut in which he put everything he had saved from the wreck. He prayed to God for rescue, and anxiously scanned the horizon every day to signal any passing ship.

One day he returned to his hut and to his horror found it in flames and all of his possessions gone. What a tragedy! Shortly after, a ship arrived. "We saw your smoke signal and hurried here," the captain explained. The survivor had only seen his burnt hut, but out of disaster, God worked a blessing. The shipwrecked man fell to his knees to thank God for the fire that caused his rescue.

Billy Graham is a world renowned evangelist and best-selling author.

STRANGE ANGELS

by Jan Winebrenner

Yes, your illness is appendicitis. But I can't do anything for
you here. You will have to go to the hospital in Shanghai,"
the doctor said.

Dick could see that he had no other choice. But he was
determined to return to Shenkiu in order to take Margaret and
the children with him. He knew his condition was critical. He
could waste no time getting to Shanghai to a hospital.

Part of the trip would have to be made by ricksha. That
wouldn't have been so bad except for several obstacles. It was
winter and there was snow on the ground. Two rickshas would
be needed to carry Dick and his wife and their two children.
Then there were military lines to cross.

Just before they left they bowed their heads. "Lord,"
Margaret prayed, "You know we need milk for our babies and
men to open doors—doors that will take us through the
Chinese lines and on to Shanghai. Lord, let us learn the truth
of Your promise, 'The angel of the Lord encampeth around
them that fear Him.'"

Then they settled into the rickshas. Baby Margaret Anne
snuggled close to her mother in one ricksha while Dick held

little John in the other. With blankets and robes tucked in around them, they were ready. But it was slow and tedious travel. On the evening of the second day they arrived at the headquarters of the defending Chinese army on the southern bank of the Sand River.

Dick went to see the commanding officer to request permission to cross the battle lines.

"Fool!" bellowed the commander. "You are crazy! The Japanese will attack at any moment, and it will mean certain death to step across the lines into no-man's land. Between here and the Japanese army there are groups of bandits."

The belligerent commander was sure such a description would discourage the strange American family that wanted to cross the windswept plains beyond the Sand River. But Dick was not easily dissuaded, and the officer finally gave in. He wrote the paper giving permission to cross the river and enter the war zone.

As he left the general's headquarters, the son of a fine Christian saw him. He recognized Dick immediately.

"Pastor," he greeted Dick. "Can I do something to help you?"

It was a strange offer coming from a young man who had refused to accept his father's faith. He had broken his father's heart with his life of wickedness and even now was engaged in smuggling opium across the lines.

The youth led the family through the streets to a little mud lean-to. There were no doors or windows, but it was shelter.

Just at daylight the smuggler led them to the edge of the Sand River where they found a boat he had chartered for them. They were taken across the river and several miles into no-man's land. As the smuggler left them to return to his river headquarters, Dick and Margaret knew they had much to be thankful for: they were alive and God had provided an angel in the form of a smuggler who had led them through many dangerous hours.

The setting sun on the second evening across no-man's land found them tired, discouraged, and running out of both food and milk. As they stopped outside an abandoned house in a large deserted village, Dick wondered, as he had many times that day, "*Do you see us, Lord? Do you have any more angels for us?*"

They carried their few things into the house and began to settle down for the night. Dick was on his knees rummaging through one of the suitcases when a rough voice behind him shouted, "Chi-lai, Stand up!"

Even before he turned around Dick knew that they had been captured by bandits. He turned slowly and stood up. The guns he saw pointing at him confirmed his fears. He barely had a moment to draw a breath when the leader ordered his men to take the suitcases. Then in sharp, crisp barks, he demanded all of Dick's money.

Dick reached for his wallet and at the same time did what comes naturally in China—he handed him his namecard and asked, "What is your honorable name?"

The simple question angered the bandit.

Cursing, he demanded, "Do you want to identify me to the authorities?" Then, as suddenly as his rage had erupted it subsided and a strange look came over his face. "Why, your name is the same as mine!" he exclaimed.

Grasping at a straw, Dick said to him, "Kind sir, we are members of the same family! We are now united."

"It is true," the bandit answered in a somber voice, "you are my elder brother."

Turning to his soldiers, he ordered them to return all of the goods they were holding and see that everything was put back into place. He assured Dick he would do his duty, for Dick was his elder brother. He forgot the difference in their skin color and the national origin. They had the same surname, and that made them brothers. He ordered his men to unroll their blankets for sleep, and that night bandits and missionaries slept together.

Next morning, the "angel" provided his best man as a guide for Dick and Margaret's journey. That afternoon the guide left them within sight of the Great Walled City after showing them that just outside the city were the Japanese lines. The little party paused and committed themselves into God's care and moved cautiously forward toward the walls of the city.

Suddenly, two Japanese sentries stood before them and shouted something at them that they could not understand. Dick took off his hat, shouted back to them in English, and slowly walked up toward the pointed guns.

The soldiers began to search their ricksha, jabbering at them in their unintelligible language. After a few minutes they moved behind the pullers, held bayonets to their backs, and ordered them to march up to the gate of the Great Walled City. At the gate a battle of words began between the guards and the sentries who had captured them. The guards had been ordered to let no one inside the gate. They were adamant; they would not open the gate.

Suddenly, the sound of galloping horses filled the air, and three Japanese officers rode up. The one in the center was a two star general. In perfect English he addressed Dick. "Where in the world did you come from?"

Dick was astonished. Then quickly he answered with his story of illness and his need to get to a hospital. As he finished his account, he added wearily, "We need rest, baths, and milk, sir. And may I ask you, sir, where did you learn such perfect English?"

Without hesitation the officer informed them that he had attended the University of Washington in 1936.

"General," Dick said, "give me the pleasure of introducing you to your fellow alumna. My wife was also at the University of Washington in 1936."

The general's face beamed with amazement and delight. He greeted Margaret warmly, promising to fulfill any requests he could. Margaret's first request was for rest and milk for her babies. The general immediately barked some orders in Japanese to his men, then turned to his fellow alumna and promised, "You shall have all that you requested. In the morning I will give you a pass to take you through Japanese lines. You will find milk at the church, for the former missionary owned a cow."

The great gates creaked open to admit the exhausted party. The people of the city gawked at the dirty little party as they passed through the streets toward the Christian church. The cow was milked, water was heated for baths, and they spent a restful night in the mud and straw church. The next morning the general provided the promised pass and an escort to take them safely outside the city.

The last leg of their journey was in sight: a train ride to Shanghai. As he relaxed into the seat of the train, Dick closed his eyes and remembered with amazement the different "angels" God had sent in response to Margaret's trusting prayer at the beginning of their journey.

THE MEN WITH THE BIBLES

Author unknown
Submitted by Joe Aldrich

In a village in the mountains of Iran, a number of new believers heard that they could find out more about Jesus if they could get the book Christians called the Bible. One night, a man had a dream that if he went down to the highway, some men would come by who would be able to give him a Bible.

The next day, he gathered a little offering of money from among the believers in the village, and made his way down the mountainside to the highway that ran through the area. He sat on a rock and began to wait.

Some time later, two men in a car just "happened" to pick up a shipment of Bibles across the border. They were driving along the same highway when the steering on their car suddenly locked. They couldn't move it more than an inch.

They finally nudged the steering wheel just enough to get the car over to the side of the road. They got out and put up the hood to figure out what was wrong. A man sitting on a nearby rock called out to them, "Are you the men with the Bibles?"

Stunned that this man should know, they admitted, "Well, yes, we do have Bibles." The old man gave them all the money he had collected, bought as many Bibles as he could, and made his way back to the village.

The men with the Bibles then went back to determine what was wrong with their car, but could find nothing. They shrugged their shoulders, got in, and drove away.

Joe Aldrich is the former president of Multnomah College and Seminary, Portland, Oregon..

MIRACLE IN THE DETAILS

by Jerry Jenkins

I f Scott Thom ever needed evidence of the hand of God in
everyday circumstances, he got it in the spring of 1990.

Scott, then associate pastor of Calvary Chapel in West
Covina, California was making a call with a colleague at Queen
of the Valley Hospital. A nurse asked if he would pray for the
patient behind the curtain in the other bed. "She had a stroke
and has been in a coma for several days," the nurse said. "We
don't expect her to last much longer."

Scott slipped into a chair by the elderly woman's bed, idly
noticing on the monitor that her heart rate was steady in the
low 70s. He lifted her limp hand and read the name off the
wristband. "Barbara," he said quietly, "I know that sometimes
people who are comatose can hear and understand what is
going on around them, so I'm going to talk to you that way.

"Normally a pastor would read something comforting, like
Psalm 23. But I don't know you, Barbara, or where you stand
with God. Before I read Psalm 23, I'd like to read Psalm 22.
Before Christ can become your shepherd, you have to know
how much He loves you and how He became that shepherd.

Scott began to read: "My God, my God, why have you

forsaken me? Why are you so far from saving me, so far from the words of my groaning?" Before he got to the third verse, Scott felt the fierce grasp of the old woman and was startled to see her heart rate race to more than 100. She opened her eyes and cried out hoarsely through the half of her mouth that still functioned, "He has not forsaken me! I've forsaken Him!"

Afraid the woman would expire any moment, Scott spoke earnestly. "Barbara, let me share something with you from the New Testament." He turned to John 6: "'The work of God is this: to believe in the one he has sent'.... Jesus declared, 'I am the bread of life. He who comes to me will never go hungry, and he who believes in me will never be thirsty'" (vv. 29,35).

"Barbara, would you like to come to God, to never thirst and hunger again?"

"Yes," she managed.

Scott explained how she could repent of sin and ask Christ to save her. "Would you like to pray with me and do that?"

"Yes!"

And so he led her in prayer. As soon as she finished, she released her grip and grew calm. Her pulse dropped to normal.

Scott moved to help his colleague finish with the other patient. As they were leaving, he ducked back into Barbara's area to say good-bye. She had slipped back into her coma.

The next day Scott had to meet with a young man to arrange a funeral. The man was angry. He had called earlier to ask someone to visit his mother in the hospital, and no one had gone. Later, they concluded that he had mistakenly called a different church.

"I'm pretty sure my mother was not a believer," he said. "She died last night after a stroke and several days in a coma."

Scott looked up. "Was she at Queen of the Valley?"

"Yes."

"Room 203?" The young man nodded.

"I was there," Scott said. "And do I have a story for you." Both wept as they planned the funeral and graveside service.

A couple of days later, when Scott showed up at the funeral home, he was asked, "What are you doing here? The husband has changed the arrangements to graveside only!"

Scott raced to the cemetery, but arrived late, and another funeral procession had been put in line ahead of Barbara's. The rest of the family was bitter, and the husband would not speak with Scott.

Four other relatives had not heard of the change either, and they didn't arrive until an hour-and-a-half later when the graveside service finally began. Scott told the story of his amazing encounter with the dying woman and asked if anyone else wished to receive Christ as Savior.

Two of the four late arrivals raised their hands. Later, the husband received Christ, and Scott eventually officiated at his funeral.

It just so happened that Scott was at Queen of the Valley.

It just so happened that the nurse asked him to pray with a dying woman in the same room.

It just so happened that he selected Psalm 22.

And that the woman's son called the church for a minister.

And that the burial was late.

It just so happened.

Jerry Jenkins is a writer in residence at Moody Bible Institute, and author of more than fifty books.

Miracles of

PROVISION

There is nothing irrational about believing that the God
who made the world can still intrude creatively into it.

J.I. Packer

Miracles of
PROVISION

I s it meal time yet? If so, you're in luck: McDonald's, Wendy's, Burger King, Taco Bell…they're everywhere, ready to satisfy your slightest hunger pang. Tired? No problem. There's a Motel 6, Motel 8, Hampton Inn, Holiday Inn, Hilton Inn…shelter on almost every corner. No matter what your desire, there's someone around who can satisfy it. The basic needs of life are all covered.

Then again, maybe they're not.

On the surface, the average American seems to have it all. But if most of our needs are met, then why are so many of us lonely? Looking for a better life? Chasing rainbows?

Today, more and more people are realizing that life isn't about what we own. To the spiritually unfulfilled, life is a vacuum that the modern lifestyle just can't satisfy. God desires not only to provide our basic physical necessities, but to fill our deepest spiritual longings. He is in the business of caring for his people. He reaches down into the paths of life and provides answers, help, fulfillment, and meaning.

And quite often, he does so through those unusual happenings we call…miracles.

Guiding Signs

by Dawn Raffel

Marlene Wiechman has never *seen* angels but she believes their intervention saved her six-year-old daughter. "Emily had a stroke at seven months, and she's partially handi-capped," Wiechman says. "Last year, we went on vacation with my parents to Yellowstone National Park. On the way home, driving through Wyoming, Emily said she didn't feel well. She started vomiting, and her eyes weren't focusing. We needed to get her to a hospital, but the nearest town, Rock Springs, was seventy miles away. Emily kept getting worse, and as we approached Rock Springs, I prayed we'd find help quickly. Just then, we saw a blue-and-white hospital sign. There were three or four more signs that led us straight to the emergency room."

A doctor quickly diagnosed Emily as having a seizure and stabilized her with anticonvulsants. After the crisis was over, Wiechman mentioned that the signs had been a lifesaver. "The doctor looked at me and said, 'What signs?' He said he traveled that road every day, and there were no hospital signs. But all four adults in our van had seen them. We went back and looked again. They were gone. I called someone at the chamber of commerce, who said there had never been any hospital signs on that route," says Wiechman. "I believe they were put there for us by God or his angels."

A SMALL GIRL'S PRAYER

by Helen Roseveare

One night I had worked hard to help a mother in the labor ward; but in spite of all we could do, she died, leaving us with a tiny premature baby and a crying two-year-old daughter. We would have difficulty keeping the baby alive, as we had no incubator (we had no electricity to run an incubator!) and no special feeding facilities. Although we lived on the equator, nights were often chilly with treacherous drafts. One student midwife went for the box we had for such babies and the cotton wool the baby would be wrapped in. Another went to stoke up the fire and fill a hot water bottle. She came back shortly, in distress, to tell me that in filling the bottle, it had burst. Rubber perishes easily in tropical climates.

"And it is our last hot water bottle!" she exclaimed.

As in the West it is no good crying over spilled milk, so in Central Africa it might be considered no good crying over burst water bottles. They do not grow on trees, and there are no drugstores down forest pathways.

"All right," I said. "Put the baby as near the fire as you safely can; sleep between the baby and the door to keep it free from drafts. Your job is to keep the baby warm."

The following noon, as I did most days, I went to have prayers with any of the orphanage children who chose to gather with me. I gave the youngsters various suggestions of things to pray about and told them about the tiny baby. I explained our problem about keeping the baby warm enough, mentioning the hot water bottle. The baby could so easily die if it got chills. I also told them of the two-year-old sister, crying because her mother had died.

During the prayer time, one ten-year-old girl, Ruth, prayed with the usual blunt conciseness of our African children.

"Please, God," she prayed, "send us a water bottle. It'll be no good tomorrow, God, as the baby'll be dead, so please send it this afternoon."

While I gasped inwardly at the audacity of the prayer, she added by way of corollary, "And while You are about it, would You please send a dolly for the little girl so she'll know You really love her?"

As often with children's prayers, I was put on the spot. Could I honestly say, "Amen"? I just did not believe that God could do this. Oh, yes, I know that He can do everything. The Bible says so. But there are limits, aren't there? And I had some very big "buts." The only way God could answer this particular prayer would be by sending me a parcel from the homeland. I had been in Africa for almost four years at that time, and I had never, ever received a parcel from home; anyway, if anyone did send me a parcel, who would put in a hot water bottle? I lived on the equator!

Halfway through the afternoon, while I was teaching in the nurses' training school, a message was sent that there was a car at my front door. By the time I reached home, the car had gone, but there, on the verandah, was a large twenty-two pound parcel. I felt tears pricking my eyes. I could not open the parcel alone, so I sent for the orphanage children. Together we pulled off the string, carefully undoing each knot. We folded the

paper, taking care not to tear it unduly. Excitement was mount-
ing. Some thirty or forty pairs of eyes were focused on the large
cardboard box.

From the top, I lifted out brightly colored, knitted jerseys.
Eyes sparkled as I gave them out. Then there were the knitted
bandages for the leprosy patients, and the children looked a little
bored! Then came a box of mixed raisins and sultanas—that
would make a nice batch of buns for the weekend. Then, as I
put my hand in again, I felt the…could it really be? I grasped it
and pulled it out—yes, a brand-new, rubber hot water bottle!

I cried. I had not asked God to send it; I had not truly
believed that He could.

Ruth was in the front row of the children. She rushed forward crying out, "If God has sent the bottle, He must have sent
the dolly, too!"

Rummaging down to the bottom of the box, she pulled out
the small, beautifully dressed dolly. Her eyes shone! She had
never doubted.

Looking up at me, she asked: "Can I go over with you,
Mummy, and give this dolly to that little girl, so she'll know
that Jesus really loves her?"

That parcel had been on the way for five whole months.
Packed up by my former Sunday school class, whose leader had
heard and obeyed God's prompting to send a hot water bottle,
even to the equator. And one of the girls had put in a dolly for an
African child—five months before—in answer to the believing
prayer of a ten-year-old to bring it "that afternoon."

*Helen Roseveare served as a missionary doctor in Zaire for twenty
years.*

Tornado!

by Joan Wester Anderson

It was 2:00 P.M. on a weekday in April 1974 in Louisville, Kentucky. Lynne Coates and her husband, Glynn, were enjoying an unexpected break from work, sitting on the steps of their porch. Their older sons were soon due home from school. Their youngest child, Collyn, would be at kindergarten at Southern Baptist Theological Seminary until about five.

The couple chatted comfortably for a while. Although the early spring day was calm, small thin lines of clouds rippled across the sky.

Glynn frowned. "Look at the sky. The last time I saw one like that was when I was twelve, when a tornado hit."

Louisville was part of the Midwest's Tornado Alley, and the weather service routinely issued tornado warnings or watches, especially in the spring. "I think we had all gotten a little blasé about tornadoes," Lynne admits now. "I certainly didn't expect to see one."

But she did. The sky got darker, the wind picked up, and Lynne began to feel apprehensive. The two older boys came home, and as the tornado sirens began, Lynne made preparations to go into the basement. Glynn, however, hunted up his camera. "If I climb high enough," he told Lynne as he hoisted himself into the tree in their front yard, "I ought to be able to get some great pictures."

"Are you crazy?" Lynne screamed at him over the rapidly rising wind. "I just heard on the radio that Brandenburg has been leveled. Get into the basement! It's really happening!"

The family huddled together underground, listening to the roar that sounded like a train bearing down on the house, and later, the pounding rain. Everyone's thoughts centered on Collyn. Was he safe? Why hadn't they gone earlier to pick him up? But who could have guessed that this time there would be a real tornado?

In just minutes the storm had passed, and the family came out of the basement. Their neighborhood seemed relatively untouched, except for occasional debris and some downed power lines. "I'm going over to the seminary to get Collyn," Glynn announced, and left immediately. They would all feel better once their youngest child was with them.

Lynne gathered the older boys, and they gave thanks to God for bringing them through the storm. Then she found a portable radio and turned it on.

They listened to reports of the damage. And then they heard that the tornado had passed directly over the seminary. One of the buildings had lost its roof.

"Oh, Dear God, Collyn!" Lynne cried, and she flew to the telephone. She dialed the number of Collyn's kindergarten, but all she heard was the popping and crackling sounds that occur when a line is out of order. If the tornado had indeed gone in that direction, there must be a lot of damage, she realized. It was possible that telephone lines were down. But she had to know if Collyn was all right! And what was keeping Glynn? An ominous feeling settled within her heart. The seminary was only a fifteen-minute drive. Glynn should have been back before now.

Lynne couldn't have known that Glynn's route took him directly into the midst of the damage. What should have taken fifteen minutes would eventually be a two-hour trip, as he wended his way around uprooted trees, rescue vehicles, fallen wires, houses dumped helter-skelter, and, perhaps worst of all, people wandering the streets in a daze. The storm had virtually destroyed a three-thousand-acre park of old trees next to the seminary, and Glynn had to park many blocks away from Collyn's building. There was no way to drive through the devastation.

At home, Lynne tried again and again to phone the seminary kindergarten, but the number wouldn't ring. Instead, she would hear clicks, then the phone would fall silent. She grew more and more distraught, and both children began to cry. *God, I can't stand any more of this,* she prayed. *You're the only one who can help us now. Please watch over Collyn and the other children, and keep them safe.*

Once more, Lynne tried to phone. After a few clicks, the phone suddenly started to ring! A calm, pleasant-sounding woman then picked it up. "Don't worry," she answered Lynne's frantic questions. "The children are fine. They were all taken to another building before the storm. Their teachers will stay with them as long as it takes the parents to pick them up."

Lynne hung up, and she and the boys shouted for joy. Collyn was safe! They would just have to sit and wait.

More than two hours later, Glynn and Collyn arrived. Glynn told Lynne that he had found a sign posted on Collyn's building door, telling parents where to go to collect their children. He had gone to the building and found Collyn there safe. Collyn had no memory of the tornado at all, except for noticing a bent weather vane on top of one of the buildings.

Lynne accompanied Collyn to his classroom on his first day

back to school. She wanted to get the name of the woman who had relieved her fear on the telephone. "I'd like to thank her," she explained to Collyn's teacher.

The teacher looked at Lynne in bewilderment. "But you couldn't have spoken with anyone," she said.

"Oh, but I did," Lynne assured her. "You can ask my older boys. I was frantic until this woman assured me that Collyn was fine."

"Mrs. Coates, that would have been impossible," the teacher insisted. "We put a sign on the door, locked the building, and moved the children before the tornado struck. There wasn't anyone here.

"And don't forget—our phone lines were destroyed. No call could have gotten through—or been answered."

Angels have been called our "companions in a storm." The Coates family knows, in a special way, what that lovely promise means.

When the Rain Came

by Una Roberts Lawrence

1937

There was a little pause, and then she took up her story:

"All of you know that Father Carter and I lived in Kansas many years, where he was a pioneer minister. We went out there from Boston when the country was new. Many wonderful stories were told us of the rich soil and favorable climate of the new country. No mention was made of droughts and famines. So when we left Boston we carried with us the savings of many other people for investment in this great new country. Father's sterling integrity made it a safe risk.

"Father called our first house a blister on the plain, and truly it did look insignificant on the great expanse of rolling prairie. Father rode miles and miles to reach his appointments, and I was often lonely while he was gone. But when planting time came we were both too busy and too thrilled by the bigness of it all to feel homesick. All we had to do was plant and wait, and let the Lord give us the increase.

"But as the days went by and the young crops grew, I heard anxious discussion of the rains that must come if we were to see our wheat mature. The season wore on with no rain. The grain grew rapidly, and then began to dwindle and wither. There before our eyes hundreds of acres of precious wheat burned to yellow wisps. We heard then of other times of drought; and realized that before leaving home we had not heard all about this country.

"But we set to work with high hopes for the next year. We told each other bravely that 'next year' we would make such a bumper crop that our barns would be full, and there would be a generous return to our home folk on their investment. No blue letters were written back to Boston.

"The next year came—and with it the same story. Dry winds swept the waving fields of green, and blasted and withered them. We were heartsick that time, but we went out and borrowed money for the next year's crop. It was all we could do. Our living and the saving of other people were tied up in the chance that the third year would bring an abundance of rain to the thirsty land.

"That third year was an anxious time. Father had the New England conscience, and felt heavily the responsibility for the investment of other people's money. It would disgrace him if he failed to make returns on our use of it. Days went by, and no rain came. Father grew more and more silent, and began to take long walks in the sun. I was anxious for him, for I felt that he was suffering keenly. I had believed that the Lord had sent us to our new home, but now I began to doubt.

"One day I overheard a conference of several wheat growers. They agreed that all signs pointed to a continuance of the drought, and they were trying to lay plans to relieve those who were hardest hit by the failure. I knew no relief could come to us; for not only was our fortune involved, but the fortunes of those who had trusted us.

"So I decided that I would take the matter to the Lord. I was desperate, and in my despair I said I would know if the Lord was a refuge in time of trouble. I would test Him and know if He cared for His people.

"I put on my best dress, a black satin left from earlier days, and very solemnly went to the parlor. I took the great Bible down from the table and laid it on the chair, and kneeling down, bowed my head on it. At first the words would not come, but soon I was pouring out my heart to God. I felt that He was very near me and was hearing me. I pleaded for help from this shame that would be ours if this crop were a failure. I prayed for rain, floods of it.

"After a while I felt a calm in my heart like the lull after a storm, but that was not enough. I wanted something more tangible than a feeling for an answer. I asked for a sign, a definite certain sign. In my daring I asked the Lord to show me from His Word that my prayer was answered. Bowing my head I opened my Bible without looking to see where. The leaves dropped back and settled in place. Not till they had ceased to flutter did I dare look at the words.

"This is what I read: 'Fear not, O land; be glad and rejoice: for the LORD will do great things.…For he hath given you the former rain moderately, and he will cause to come down for you the rain, the former rain, and the latter rain, in the first month. And the floors shall be full of wheat, and the vats shall overflow with wine and oil. And I will restore to you the years that the locust hath eaten, the cankerworm, and the caterpillar, and the palmerworm, my great army which I sent among you. And ye shall eat in plenty, and be satisfied, and praise the name of the LORD your God, that hath dealt wondrously with you: and my people shall never be ashamed' (Joel 2:21–26, KJV).

"I read no further. I arose from my knees with a feeling of exaltation. I had met the Lord and He had given me the sign of

His presence. He had said, 'My people shall never be put to shame.' Was it not enough?"

There was a bit of a pause as the young people waited for her to go on.

"And did the rain come?" The question was not of doubt but of eager interest.

"I met Father as I left the room. I remember afterward how surprised he looked at seeing me so dressed up.

"'Rain is coming,' I said very calmly. He looked at me keenly and then with his arm around me he drew me to a chair. 'Are you tired, dear?' he asked. I saw that he thought the strain had proved too much for me. I smiled at him and with happiness thrilling my whole being, I said, 'I know, John, that rain is coming!' and I told him the whole story. He went with me into the parlor where the Bible still lay open at the words spoken by Joel so long ago. He read them in silence, then bowed his head a moment with me.

"'Come, let us go out,' he said. We passed one of the ranch hands in the passage and he started as I called to him that the rain was coming. I saw him shake his head anxiously at me. Out into the open we went, Father and I, down the long lines of drooping wheat, until we stood where the house could not be seen, only the great waving expanse of grain.

"'It looks like a floor of wheat,' I said. We stood some time in silence. Then Father said reverently, "'And my people shall never be put to shame." Praise His name!' Back to the house we went. Never for one minute did either of us doubt the word we had been given. Rain was coming! Dark came on in midafternoon, and great excitement spread among the field hands. A man came running in shouting, 'A cloud is coming up! It's going to rain!' I shall never forget Father's voice as he answered, 'Yes, we have known it since early this afternoon.'

"And it rained! The floods for which I prayed. It sounded on the roof like a paean of praise to the God who answers prayer, and echoed in our hearts again and again, the precious promise, 'My people shall never be put to shame.' Father looked out on the descending torrents, and with a smile I heard him repeat, 'The former and the latter rains—in just measure.'"

No one spoke for a while. Then the boy found expression for his conclusion. "That was God!" he said, as if he had just found Him for himself. Frank nodded assent.

"And faith in God," added Carrie in a tone that told better than words that she had found faith, never to lose it again.

MARY'S SECRET LIST

by Barb Marshall

Missionaries are extraordinary individuals. Good friends of ours, Mary and Mike Corbett, were on the mission field for ten years, in Mexico and Bolivia. I've heard fascinating stories of what they experienced while living in Third World countries. The following is an incident from when they were at Kingsway Bible Institute in Texas, a nine-month missionary language school.

"We left Ohio without any pledge support," Mary said. "We were just relying on anything people might happen to send to us. Mike had a part-time job but with school expenses, we were very low on food. We ate a lot of pancakes!

"One day I felt impressed to write out a grocery list: it was like a 'wish' list. If I went to the store (if I had the money), what would I need? I meticulously wrote out the list and then went off to school. I didn't tell anyone about it: most of our friends were in the same position we were—living on faith and doing something they had never done before in their lives!

"That afternoon, when we were studying at home, we

heard a knock on the door. By the time we opened it, nobody was there. On the doorstep sat two bags of groceries. One by one I took all the items out of the bags—every single thing had been on my list. The only missing item was bread. I was in awe!

"Later, when Mike went to his job, a person he worked with arrived with a station-wagon-load of day-old bread! That night he came home with four loaves of bread. I just cried; I totally lost it! I felt like God was saying, 'Nothing is too insignificant that I don't care about it.' It was God's way of saying, 'You're important to me!'

"We never did find out who did it, but whomever it was had to have been tuned in to the Holy Spirit. Nobody had seen my list!"

PROVIDENCE SPRING

by J. C. Sills

Demetrius Lower of St. Louis was a soldier in the second regiment of New York Cavalry during the American Civil War. He was taken prisoner in the battle, and was confined for a time in Libby Prison in Richmond. Later, with many other prisoners, he was transferred to the military prison at Andersonville, in western Georgia. This prison was an open field on the side of a hill. It contained about twenty-two acres enclosed by a stockade of stout timbers twelve or fourteen feet high. Above were guards who watched the prison.

A small stream of water ran through the prison at the foot of the hill, which was to furnish the prisoners with the water they needed. This served the purpose well enough while the prison was new, with but few men in it. But daily there came more and more. During the war more than forty-nine thousand entered. With large numbers within the stockade, the prison litter moving down the hillside filled and stagnated the little stream. Soon under the burning summer sun the prisoners began to suffer for water to drink. Day by day their thirst became more terrible. Many were dying, with no help nor hope in sight.

In the prison were Christian men who knew that God could help and that He answered prayer. When their sufferings became intense they cried to Him for water. Then, as the psalmist said, "He heard them in their trouble and delivered them out of their distresses." In the night there came a tremendous rain such as is rarely seen, flooding all the ground. Early in the morning to their great joy the prisoners found that a strong spring had burst out on the hillside, flowing down in a copious stream. Deliverance had come. Their suffering and thirst were over. It was so clearly the miraculous work of God that they named it "Providence Spring."

The Civil War is ended and almost forgotten. The prison is no more, and those associated with its scenes have gone the way of all the earth, but the spring is still there. When the summer drought parches the country round and dries up other streams, it flows on in cool and sparkling freshness, a permanent memorial of God's infinite goodness and faithfulness in answering prayer.

The prison grounds are now enclosed and embellished, and the spring is now encased in masonry in which is inserted a bronze tablet on which is inscribed the significant name, "Providence Spring."

THE BRIDGE THAT WASN'T THERE

by Howard Foltz

I have ministered all over the world and heard stories that seemed to have no logical explanation outside of God's intervention. One story in particular stands out.

Ben Taylor, a colleague, told me about a trip that he had taken to a church in the mountains above La Ceiba, Honduras. His driver was Tito Rodriques, the national superintendent of churches for a Latin American denomination. Late in the afternoon, Ben related, Tito stopped abruptly in the middle of the road, saying that he had something to show his passengers.

Ben exited the car and found himself in front of a 30-foot wooden span that crossed a deep chasm.

Tito said that he had been on this road a month earlier on his way to a preaching engagement. The weather had been horrible. The region had endured a three-day storm because of a hurricane. Tito had made the trip anyway, and when he arrived in the village, everyone was surprised to see him.

"How did you get here?" they asked.

"I came on the road from La Ceiba," he replied.

"That's impossible!" the villagers told him. "The bridge washed out last night."

Tito told them that the bridge must have already been repaired. He could tell, he said, because the wood was still white and unweathered.

"No, Tito. The bridge is gone," they told him. A few of the villagers accompanied him to the chasm to prove their point. And they were right—there was no bridge. Yet Tito had crossed the chasm safely, driving across a bridge made of brand-new wood.

Howard Foltz is professor of global evangelism, School of Divinity, Regent University.

AN UNLIKELY RAIN

by Doris Sanford

My parents were missionaries in China during a time when it was unpopular to be an American and unsafe to be a missionary. As the Communist soldiers invaded farther and farther into China, they soon reached the village in the far north where my parents and my twin and I lived. Our older brother and sister were away at a Christian boarding school on the coast of China.

It started with mostly just rumors of danger, but soon there were actual threats against the believers in the church my father pastored. Bibles were piled and burned in the village—an attempt to intimidate Chinese Christians and convince them to renounce their faith. Church services were forbidden and the underground gatherings began. When there was direct confrontation and a command to leave the foreign God, Christians were tortured and publicly shot or beheaded.

One afternoon when my father had gone to another village to encourage Christians there, and my mother was home alone with my brother and me, there was the sudden noise of soldiers shouting in the courtyard. They demanded that my mother come out. The three of us obeyed.

Once in the courtyard, we were commanded to dig three shallow graves while they pointed guns at our heads. When the task was done, my brother and I were each roped to one of our mother's legs and her hands were tied behind her back.

The soldier in charge shouted in Chinese, "Renounce your foreign God and we will set you free!" Mother said, "We cannot deny the one true God. He is more powerful than your guns and if He chooses He can speak the word and we will be safe from your guns. Or, if He chooses, we will go to heaven to live with Him forever, beginning today."

The leader raised his gun and the others followed. At that moment the sky suddenly darkened and crashed with thunder and lightning! My mother said that in the northern interior of China, thunder and lightning were unheard of. Snow and ice, yes, but torrential downpours along with flashes of light and deafening thunder, *never!*

The men trampled themselves in their eagerness to escape, convinced that the God of the missionaries had spoken. My mother smiled and wiggled out of wet ropes to take two young children back to the house for a cup of hot tea.

Doris Sanford is the author of more than a dozen books, and a teacher of psychiatric nursing.

FAITH AND ACTION

by Henry T. Blackaby and Claude V. King

Our church in Saskatoon was growing and needed more space. We sensed God leading us to start a building program, even though we had only $749 in the building fund. The building was going to cost $220,000. We didn't have the foggiest notion how to do it.

We did much of the work to save on labor costs. Still, halfway through that building program, we were $100,000 short. Those dear, dear people looked to their pastor to see if I believed that God would do what He had called us to do. God put a confidence in my heart that the God who was leading us would show us how to do it.

God began providing the necessary funds. We were about $60,000 short toward the end. We had been expecting some money from a Texas foundation. Delay after delay came that we could not understand. One day, for two hours, the currency rate for the Canadian dollar hit the lowest point ever in its history. That was exactly the time the Texas foundation wired the money to Canada. You know what that did? It gave us $60,000 more than we would have gotten otherwise. Then the dollar went back up.

Co-authors of Experiencing God, *Henry Blackaby is the Director of Prayer and Spiritual Awakening, Southern Baptist Convention Home Mission Board and Claude King is a writer for the adult training section of the Southern Baptist Sunday School Board's Discipleship Training Department.*

My Encourager

by Kenneth Taylor

We had read over and over again to our youngest children (different years, different children) all the available books of Bible stories geared to three- and four-year-olds. Some were on the life of Christ, others on Old Testament heroes such as Joseph or Daniel, but I could not find a book that covered the entire Bible for very young children.

Finally the thought occurred to me to try writing such a book myself. I experimented with the idea and wrote some half-page stories that could match pictures in the Sunday school papers the children brought home. I would hold a child on my lap, show the picture, and read the Bible story I had written about the picture. I asked a few questions and could tell whether the story was understood. My children's response to the experiment was good.

The material was handwritten, so I arranged with the typing pool at Moody Bible Institute to type as much as I had written. But part way through the Bible I became discouraged, and wondered whether to continue with the project. A few days later a young woman stopped me in the hallway and told me she had been typing my manuscript and was very enthusiastic about it. This greatly encouraged me, so I decided to finish writing the book. Since this was an important decision, I went the next day to the typing pool to thank the young woman for her enthusiasm. I didn't see her, so I asked the supervisor whether the person who typed my manuscript was away for the day.

The supervisor looked puzzled. "Katherine typed it," she said. "She's right over there." But the person she pointed to wasn't the one I had talked to in the hallway. I described her to the supervisor, but she said no, all her typists were there in the room. And certainly none of them was my encourager.

I believe it was an angel God sent the previous day, to tell me to go ahead. That book is *The Bible in Pictures for Little Eyes*, published in 1956, and there are now more than a million copies in print. I thank God for sending His angel that day in the hallway of the seventh floor of Moody Bible Institute.

Note from the editor: The Bible in Pictures for Little Eyes *has been printed in fifty-four languages and is listed by* Publisher's Weekly *as one of the all-time best-selling children's books.*

Kenneth Taylor is founder and chairman of the board for Tyndale House Publishers, Inc., and is best known for his para-phrase, The Living Bible.

THE MUSIC BOX

by Sherry Angel

One night, Jean Vistica heard music coming from her back bedroom. When she went to investigate, the music stopped, but she knew it had come from a music box on her bureau that hadn't been wound or played in months. Then she smelled something strange and discovered that an electrical outlet next to the bureau was warm to the touch. This prompted her to turn off the electricity and call firefighters, who found a problem in the wiring that posed a serious fire hazard.

"The problem arose during the half-hour between my getting home and going to bed. It could have occurred at any time during the day or after I was asleep, but it didn't," she writes. "I was overwhelmed by love from a protective God...there was absolutely no doubt in my mind as to Who caused my music box to play."

ONE THOUSAND DOLLARS SHORT

by Bernie May

I was called out of a meeting in Oklahoma to take an urgent phone message from Forrey Zander, who directs the regional office of Wycliffe Bible Translators in Chicago. Forrey was excited. He had been talking with a young woman from Asia who had just completed her master's degree in communications at Wheaton College. Since foreign missionaries are no longer allowed in her country, this young woman, Thangi, had planned to return to her homeland in some missionary capacity.

Thangi had contacted Forrey in our Chicago office. He, in turn, had suggested she apply to the Summer Institute of Linguistics school in Dallas—to work on another master's degree, this time in linguistics. It was now one week before deadline and Thangi was still $1000 short. Forrey was calling, asking if I could raise some money for this critical need.

I was certain there was enough money—in some budget—to send Thangi to graduate school in Dallas so she could return to her own people. All I would have to do was change some priorities. But I also knew that that would be trusting in my own ability. I felt God was asking me to trust Him.

"I can't treat her in a special way," I told Forrey. "But if God wants her in school this week, we can trust Him to locate and provide the funds. I will do two things. I'll pray about it. And if anyone approaches me and says they have one thousand dollars, to help train a national translator, I'll direct the money to Thangi.

I could hear the air escaping from Forrey's punctured balloon. But since he also understands what it means to trust God and not self, he agreed to my terms. He contacted Thangi, told her of the decision to trust God, and received her enthusiastic approval. She, too, understood the principle.

The next day I had lunch with a wealthy man who could easily have written out a check for one thousand dollars to send Thangi to school. All I had to do was use some marketing and sales ability I had learned a long time ago and I knew he would give the money. But I had no leading to ask for money for Thangi. I left the luncheon feeling guilty, but I knew I was right to wait on God.

Two days later I was flying my plane from Oklahoma back to California. The weather was bad over the southern route, so I flew home by way of Colorado. I knew my friends Henry and Marcia Stuart from Dallas were probably vacationing at their cabin near Crested Butte. I needed gas anyway, so when I stopped over, I gave them a call.

Henry was delighted to hear my voice and drove over and picked me up at the airport to take me out to his house. I was just getting ready to sit down on the porch and drink a glass of tea when Henry spoke up.

"Bernie, I'm glad you stopped by. I've been thinking about the work carried on by Wycliffe Bible Translators. It seems you ought to try to find some Christian nationals and begin training them to help with the translation. If you ever find anyone like that, I'd like to invest one thousand dollars to help with their education."

I began to laugh. "Let me tell you about Thangi," I said.

By the time I had finished my story, Marcia had brought Henry the checkbook and I had the money in hand.

Bernie May is on staff with Wycliffe Bible Translators.

Right on Top

by Mother Teresa

A man came to our house and said, "My only child is dying! The doctor has prescribed a medicine that you can only get in England." Now, I have permission from our government to store life-saving medicines that are gathered from all over the country. We have many people who go from house to house and gather leftover medicines. And they bring them to us and we give them to our poor people. We have thousands of people who come to our dispensaries. While we were talking, a man came in with a basket of medicines.

I looked at that basket of medicines: right on the top was the very medicine the first man needed for his dying child! If it had been underneath, I wouldn't have seen it.

If it had come earlier or later, I would not have remembered. It came just in time.

I stood in front of that basket and I was thinking, "There are millions of children in the world, and God is concerned with that little child in the slums of Calcutta. To send that man at that very moment! To put the medicine right on the top, so I could see it!

He would do the same thing for each one of us."

Mother Teresa is a world renowned humanitarian ministering to the poor in India.

Miracles and

ANGELS

I'M MORE CONVINCED THAN EVER THAT ANGELS ARE FAR MORE INVOLVED

IN OUR WORLD THAN MOST OF US REALIZE.

I BELIEVE THEY CERTAINLY DO INTERVENE HERE, BOTH VISIBLY AND INVISIBLY.

DAVID JEREMIAH

Miracles and
ANGELS

Have you ever seen an angel? Nope, sorry. TV angels don't count. I'm talking about the kind of angels that are so real and awesome and terrifying, they have to start each conversation with: "Don't be afraid…."

As far as I know, I have never seen an angel. The truth is, though, I may have and not even known it. Maybe you have, too. The Scriptures say that we have often "entertained angels unawares."

Right now you may be saying, "That's a neat trick, but I'll believe in angels when I actually *see* one." Once you apply that same argument to air or electricity, however, you'll quickly see it doesn't hold water. A thing doesn't have to be visible to exist.

Regardless of their appearance (or lack of it), angels *are* here. They carry out the wishes of their creator. They protect us and help us. There is no way to measure how often and how involved angels are in your life. One could easily be near your side right now. (No, don't look. They're usually *invisible*, remember?)

If all the invisible angels became visible, however, we would almost certainly be paralyzed by the sight. Angels are far more involved in our world than most of us think. They play a key role in God's plan for protecting us, and there are millions of them.

There are millions of amazing angel stories as well. And here are some of the best of them. Relax. Enjoy them. Open your eyes to the invisible world around you.

And don't be too worried if you feel someone reading over your shoulder....

In a Moment of Time

by Hope MacDonald

A young mother was standing at the kitchen sink washing dishes one spring morning. Their little garden was aflame with fresh jewel-like flowers, and the smell of warm clover filled the air. In a moment of time, the long, dreary winter was forgotten.

As she looked out the window into the backyard, she noticed that the garden gate had been left open. Her little three-year-old daughter, Lisa, had toddled through the gate and was sitting casually on the railroad tracks playing with the gravel. The mother's heart stopped when she saw a train coming around the bend and heard its whistle blaring persistently. As she raced from the house screaming her daughter's name, she suddenly saw a striking figure, clothed in pure white, lifting Lisa off the tracks. While the train roared past, this glorious being stood by the track with an arm around the child. Together, they watched the train go by. When the mother reached her daughter's side, Lisa was standing alone.

Hope MacDonald is a well-known speaker at retreats and churches, and author of several books.

SAFELY HOME

by Joan Wester Anderson

It was just past midnight on December 24, 1983. The Midwest was shivering through a record-breaking cold spell, complete with gale-force winds and frozen water pipes. And although our suburban Chicago household was filled with the snug sounds of a family at rest, I couldn't be a part of them, not until our twenty-one-year-old son pulled into the driveway. At the moment, Tim and his two roommates were driving home for Christmas, their first trip back since they had moved East last May. "Don't worry, Mom," Tim had reassured me over the phone last night. "We're going to leave before dawn tomorrow and drive straight through. We'll be fine!"

Kids. They do insane things. Under normal circumstances, I figured, a Connecticut-to-Illinois trek ought to take about eighteen hours. But the weather had turned so dangerously cold that radio reports warned against venturing outdoors, even for a few moments. And we had heard nothing from the travelers. Distressed, I pictured them on a desolate road. What if they ran into car problems or lost their way? And if they *had* been delayed, why hadn't Tim phoned? Restlessly I paced and prayed in the familiar shorthand all mothers know: *God, send someone to help them.*

By now, as I later learned, the trio had stopped briefly in Fort Wayne, Indiana, to deposit Don at his family home. Common sense suggested that Tim and Jim stay the rest of the night and resume their trek in the morning. But when does common sense prevail with invincible young adults? There were only four driving hours left to reach home. And although it was the coldest night in Midwest history and the highways were snowy and deserted, the two had started out again.

They had been traveling for only a few miles on a rural access road to the Indiana tollway, when they noticed that the car's engine seemed sluggish, lurching erratically and dying to ten or fifteen miles per hour. Tim glanced uneasily at Jim. "Do not—" the radio announcer intoned, "—repeat—*do not* venture outside tonight, friends. There's a record wind-chill of eighty below zero, which means that exposed skin will freeze in less than a minute." The car surged suddenly, then coughed and slowed again.

"Tim," Jim spoke into the darkness, "we're not going to stall here, are we?"

"We can't," Tim answered grimly as he pumped the accelerator. "We'd die for sure."

But instead of picking up speed, the engine sputtered, chugging and slowing again. About a mile later, at the top of a small incline, the car crawled to a frozen stop.

Horrified, Tim and Jim looked at each other in the darkened interior. They could see across the fields in every direction, but, incredibly, theirs was the only vehicle in view. For the first time, they faced the fact that they were in enormous danger. There was no traffic, no refuge ahead, not even a farmhouse light blinking in the distance. It was as if they had landed on an alien, snow-covered planet.

And the appalling, unbelievable cold! Never in Tim's life had he experienced anything so intense. They couldn't run for help; he knew that for sure. He and Jim were young and strong, but even if shelter were only a short distance away, they couldn't survive. The temperature would kill them in a matter of minutes.

"Someone will come along soon," Jim muttered, looking in every direction. "They're bound to."

"I don't think so," Tim said. "You heard the radio. Everyone in the world is inside tonight—except us."

"Then what are we going to do?"

"I don't know." Tim tried starting the engine again, but the ignition key clicked hopelessly in the silence. Bone-chilling cold penetrated the car's interior, and his feet were already growing numb. *Well, God,* he prayed, echoing my own distant plea, *You're the only one who can help us now.*

It seemed impossible to stay awake much longer…. Then, as if they had already slipped into a dream, they saw headlights flashing at the car's rear. But that was impossible. For they had seen no twin pinpricks of light in the distance, no hopeful approach. Where had the vehicle come from? Had they already died?

But no. For, miraculously, someone was knocking on the driver's side window. "Need to be pulled?" In disbelief they heard the muffled shout. But it was true. Their rescuer was driving a tow truck.

"Yes! Oh, yes, thanks!" Quickly, the two conferred as the driver, saying nothing more, drove around to the front of the car and attached chains. If there were no garages open at this hour, they would ask him to take them back to Don's house, where they could spend the rest of the night.

Swathed almost completely in a furry parka, hood and a scarf up to his eyes, the driver nodded at their request but said nothing more. He was calm, they noted as he climbed into his truck, seemingly unconcerned about the life-threatening circumstances in which he had found them. *Strange that he's not curious about us,* Tim mused, *and isn't even explaining where he came from or how he managed to approach without our seeing him....* And had there been lettering on the side of the truck? Tim hadn't noticed any. *He's going to give us a big bill, on a night like this. I'll have to borrow some money from Don or his dad....* But Tim was exhausted from the ordeal, and gradually, as he leaned against the seat, his thoughts slipped away.

They passed two locked service stations, stopped to alert Don from a pay phone, and were soon being towed back through the familiar Fort Wayne neighborhood. Hushed, Christmas lights long since extinguished and families asleep, Don's still seemed the most welcoming street they had ever been on. The driver maneuvered carefully around the cul-de-sac and pulled up in front of Don's house. Numb with cold, Tim and Jim raced to the side door where Don was waiting, then tumbled into the blessedly warm kitchen, safe at last.

"The tow truck driver, Don—I have to pay him. I need to borrow—"

"Wait a minute." Don frowned, looking past his friends through the window. "I don't see any tow truck out there."

Tim and Jim turned around. There, parked alone at the curb was Tim's car. There had been no sound in the crystal-clear night of its release from the chains, no door slam, no chug of an engine pulling away. There had been no bill for Tim to pay, no receipt to sign, no farewell or "thank you" or "Merry Christmas...." Stunned, Tim raced back down the driveway to the curb, but there were no taillights disappearing in the distance, no engine noise echoing through the silent streets, nothing at all to mark the tow truck's presence.

Then Tim saw the tire tracks traced in the windblown snowdrifts. But there was only one set of marks ringing the cul-de-sac curve. And they belonged to Tim's car....

MARCHING ORDERS

by Corrie ten Boom

When rebels advanced on a school where two hundred children of missionaries lived, they planned to kill both children and teachers. In the school they knew of the danger and therefore went to prayer. Their only protection was a fence and a couple of soldiers, while the enemy, who came closer and closer, amounted to several hundreds. When the rebels were close by, suddenly something happened: they turned around and ran away! The next day the same thing happened and again on the third day. One of the rebels was wounded and was brought to the mission hospital. When the doctor was busy dressing his wounds, he asked him: "Why did you not break into the school as you planned?" "We could not do it. We saw hundreds of soldiers in white uniforms and we became scared." In Africa soldiers never wear white uniforms, so it must have been angels!

Corrie ten Boom was a world renowned author and speaker, and survivor of Nazi concentration camps.

ON A WINTER NIGHT

by Billy Graham

D r. S.W. Mitchell, a celebrated Philadelphia neurologist, had gone to bed after an exceptionally tiring day. Suddenly he was awakened by someone knocking on his door. Opening it he found a little girl, poorly dressed and deeply upset. She told him her mother was very sick and asked him if he would please come with her. It was a bitterly cold, snowy night, and though he was bone tired, he followed the girl.

As the *Reader's Digest* reports the story, the doctor found the mother desperately ill with pneumonia. After arranging for medical care, he complimented the sick woman on the intelligence and persistence of her little daughter. The woman looked at him strangely and then said, "My daughter died a month ago." She added, "Her shoes and coat are in the clothes closet there." Dr. Mitchell, amazed and perplexed, went to the closet and opened the door. There hung the very coat worn by the little girl who had brought him to tend to her mother. It was warm and dry and could not possibly have been out in the wintry night.

Billy Graham is a world renowned evangelist and best-selling author.

INTERVENTION ON THE FRONT LINES

by David Jeremiah

Sometimes when angels intervene on the fields of human conflict, God opens the eyes of both sides to see his heavenly beings at work. In her book, *Angels*, Hope Price records two hopeless situations in World War I related by a British captain. The first occurred early in the war near Mons, France, where outnumbered British troops had been fighting for days without relief.

They had lost many men and guns, and defeat looked inevitable. Captain Cecil W. Hayward was there and tells how suddenly, in the midst of a gun battle, firing on both sides stopped. To their astonishment, the British troops saw "four or five wonderful beings, much bigger than men," between themselves and the Germans. These "men" were bare-headed, wore white robes, and seemed to float rather than stand. Their backs were to the British and their arms and hands were outstretched toward the Germans.

At that moment, the horses ridden by German calvarymen became terrified and stampeded off in every direction.

Hayward also told of another battle sometime later in World War I when matters again seemed hopeless for the

British soldiers, who were surrounded by German troops. Suddenly the heavy enemy fire stopped completely, and everything grew strangely quiet.

Then "the sky opened with a bright shining light, and figures of luminous beings appeared floating between the British and German lines."

German troops retreated in disorder, allowing the Allied forces to reform and fall back on a line of defense farther to the west.

German prisoners were taken that day, and when they were asked why they surrendered when they had the British troops surrounded, they looked amazed, saying, "But there were hosts and hosts of you!"

Hope Price comments in her book that the British government officially sponsored national days of prayer during the conflict. She believes the government's commitment to prayer played a role in the angelic intervention on behalf of the British soldiers.

Many a godly teacher has reminded us over the centuries that all that the Lord does on our behalf is in answer to someone's prayer. That surely includes sending angels to our rescue, plus opening our eyes to see them.

There must be quite a lot of intervening angels around that we just never notice—but sometimes, when the time is right, God takes the scales off our eyes so we can see them.

David Jeremiah is senior pastor of Shadow Mountain Community Church in San Diego, president of Christian Heritage College, author, founder and host of "Turning Point" radio program.

MISSED OVERALLS

by Sam Graham Humphreys

At the time, we lived on a small farm in rural Connecticut. I was walking with my three pre-school age sons down the many paths that wove through the woods and pastures surrounding our farm. It had been a wonderful afternoon, and I think we were all a little giddy with the sense of "rightness" in our world. My second son, who was about three years old at the time was dashing a few feet forward and running back like a puppy when I called. As we approached our large pond, I held tightly to their little hands knowing that a disaster takes only a second. Maybe it was those few moments of physical restraint that caused him to break away from me once we were safely past the water. At any rate, he scampered off giggling. I could hear him and I could see occasional flashes of the bright red and yellow stripes on his shirt through the bends in the path and the breaks in the trees. At first, when he did not return at my call, I was only mildly concerned for we knew these paths well, and I could hear that he was not too far ahead. Nevertheless, I wanted to catch up to him quickly. Tucking the baby under one arm and taking a firmer grip on my oldest son, I walked with a faster more determined stride.

Abruptly my wayward son's giggling veered off in a direction I didn't anticipate. I paused just long enough to be certain of what I was hearing before scooping my four-year old up and running toward the sounds. My middle boy, without questions, was taking a less frequently traveled path that eventually made its way up a very steep hill into a horse pasture. I felt my panic rising. Scanning quickly as I reached the foot of the hill, my heart crashed to my toes; there was my boy scrambling like a little mountain goat about half way up. I placed the baby's hand in that of my oldest son and admonished them to stay put before racing up the hill. It was hard to believe such a little guy could move so fast. Urging him to stop the whole time, I slipped, slid, and clambered, all at the same time. Suddenly, I heard the faint yet unmistakable sound of hoof beats. Someone was riding very near us. It was not unusual for riders to bring the horses down this incline for it was a shortcut to the pond. I also knew that, because they were certainly not expecting my son to pop up over the edge, they would never be able to stop the horses in time.

Heart pounding, I doubled my efforts, praying all the while that I would reach him. It was no specific prayer, just, "Please God, please God" over and over. Everything happened at once. I lunged in a last desperate attempt to grab the back of his overalls just as he crested the hill. To my absolute horror and disbelief, I missed and fell with a crash inches from my child. Helplessly I watched, anticipating disaster. Suddenly my son flew backward away from me and landed on his bottom with a dusty thump. The rider tried frantically to stop her horse, which was now pawing and rearing exactly where my son had been only seconds before. Unaware of what nearly happened, my beloved child turned to me accusingly and scolded, "Mama, you didn't have to pull so hard. That hurt."

I scooped him up into a teary embrace and held him tight, despite his struggles to get loose, until my heart stopped pounding. The rider, her horse under control, and I gazed at each other in amazement. What exactly had happened? I hadn't touched him. There was only one possible answer. I know the guardian angels I had heard of as a child were looking out for this new generation just as they always have. When I look at my son today, nineteen years old and quite an amazing young man, I still get a catch in my throat when I think of what might have happened without that moment of divine intervention.

Sam Graham Humphry is administrative assistant for Hospice in East Connecticut.

LARGE FIERY FIGURES

by David Jeremiah

In the early 1950s, a missionary group in Kenya learned of an imminent attack on their mission by Mau Mau warriors. To defend their families as well as they could, the men put up a barbed wire barricade and turned on the few floodlights. With what few weapons they had they stood guard along the mission's perimeter, while their wives and children prayed inside.

They waited. But no attack came.

Months later a converted Mau Mau tribesman explained that just as he and his fellow warriors prepared to attack the mission from all sides, large fiery figures appeared from out of the night. They stood between the Mau Mau and the missionaries, racing in a circle around the barricade. Frightened by the sight of these creatures, the Mau Mau fled.

"The missionaries may not have seen them," Doug Connelly writes (from his book *Angels Around Us*), "but God opened the warriors' eyes to what normally would have been invisible—His band of holy angels.

David Jeremiah is senior pastor of Shadow Mountain Community Church in San Diego, president of Christian Heritage College, author, founder and host of "Turning Point" radio program.

A Voice of Warning

by Hope MacDonald

The week had been full and busy for the doctor. As he drove into his driveway that Saturday afternoon, he looked forward to putting on his old clothes, relaxing in front of the TV, and watching his favorite Buckeyes beat the Wolverines. Halfway through the game, the phone rang. There was an emergency at the hospital and he was needed immediately. He grabbed his bag and dashed out the door to his car in the driveway. He climbed in, turned on the key, and was ready to go. Suddenly he felt a strong presence standing by his open window. It was so real that he felt he could reach out and touch it. He even paused long enough to turn his head and look. Although he didn't see anything, he heard a word of warning. "Don't back out of the driveway. Get out and look behind you."

Even though the doctor was in a tremendous hurry, he felt he must obey the message. He got out of his car, walked around to the back, and there he saw the little two-year-old boy from next door. He was sitting in his new rocking chair, leaning up against the doctor's car, watching the lazy autumn clouds float by.

Hope MacDonald is a well-known speaker at retreats and churches, and author of several books.

THROUGH GATES OF SPLENDOR

by Olive Fleming Liefeld

Almost every major newspaper headlined the tragedy of the five martyred missionaries nearly fifty years ago in Ecuador. Literally thousands of young lives were changed because of their sacrifice. What the general public thought was a foolish waste of human life was to God a triumph of progress.

The following account adds a bit of conclusion to events started nearly fifty years ago. Kimo was one of the Aucas who killed the missionaries while Dawa watched from the riverbank. Rachel, the sister of one of the martyred men, eventually continued the work begun by her brother and lived among the Aucas. When Olive Fleming Leifeld and her friend Holly returned to Ecuador, Rachel served as their guide and translator.

As Jim Elliot, one of the martyred missionaries, said, "He is no fool who gives what he cannot keep to gain what he cannot lose." The five men did just that! The Auca Indians turned to God. On a return visit to the Waorani tribe of the Aucas, the group was given the details of that triumphant day—when the men died and the angels were present.

"They heard singing," Rachel said, puzzled.

"Who was singing?" I asked. "The five men?"

Rachel translated my question. Dawa's answer was, "No, their dead bodies were lying on the beach."

"So who was singing?" I repeated. But Rachel was concentrating too deeply to answer. We could only listen to the excited chatter of Dawa and Kimo and wait for a translation break. Back and forth the dialogue went, as Rachel asked questions and the Indians continued their animated descriptions.

At that point Holly, who had been sitting on a log down the beach and had heard the Indians' voices getting louder, joined us as we waited for the story to conclude. Judging by the facial expressions and the gesturing of Kimo and Dawa, we all knew they were saying something important.

Dawa pointed behind us, then swept her arm over the trees as she spoke. Something had happened over the jungle. It was too critical a time for us to break in with questions. Finally there was a pause. Rachel, herself confounded, then proceeded to tell us a story we could hardly comprehend, let alone believe.

"After the men were killed, Dawa in the woods and Kimo on the beach heard singing," Rachel said. "As they looked up over the tops of the trees they saw a large group of people. They were all singing, and it looked as if there were a hundred flashlights."

Flashlights?

Rachel explained, "This is the only word for 'bright light' that they know. But they said it was very bright and flashing. Then suddenly it disappeared."

A host of people singing? Flashing lights? What had Kimo and Dawa seen? What did the people look like? Were they talking about angels?

We looked to Rachel for an explanation. But the story surprised her as much as it did us. She had never heard this before. It was so unexpected, so far beyond our own experience.

"They must have made that up," Holly said.

"No, Holly, they wouldn't make that up," Rachel immediately replied. She had heard the Waorani tell stories for many years, and had verified their accuracy again and again.

I recalled the line from the hymn "We Rest on Thee": "When passing through the gates of pearly splendor...." It metaphorically depicts what death is like for a Christian—the grimness giving way to a beautiful scene of glory. Even though I believe that at death, the souls of Christians are transported into God's presence, I don't expect humans to be able to see this take place before their eyes. Had the Indians actually witnessed something that I only knew by faith? Like Holly, I too found it hard not to be skeptical.

I wondered if they had invented the story to gain approval. No, that was impossible. It came out far too spontaneously between the two of them. Too much planning would have been required for them to correlate their facts. We all had watched their faces and their elaborate gesturing. There was no question that they had seen *something*.

"Why haven't they told this story to you before?" I asked.

"We haven't talked about the killings for many years," Rachel reminded us. "I couldn't keep on asking questions about how they killed my brother."

We were convinced that Rachel was right: Kimo and Dawa had not made up the story. We guessed that most likely they had been terrified by the vision, and therefore did not talk about it when first questioned about the killings. Perhaps it took years of Bible teaching for them to understand what they had seen. Or possibly, the fuller knowledge of Scripture they now possess led them to embellish their account somewhat. But whatever the explanation, we knew we could not dismiss the story.

Olive Fleming Liefeld is the wife of Pete Fleming, one of the martyred missionaries, and author of Unfolding Destinies.

STRANGER AT THE GATE

by V. Raymond Edman

Mrs. Edman and I were young missionaries in the Andean highlands of the lovely little republic of Ecuador in western South America. After our marriage in the capital city of Quito, we were given our first assignment to a city whose environs had thousands of Quichua-speaking Indians. We lived on the outskirts of that city where we could reach both the Spanish-speaking citizens on the streets and in the marketplaces, and also the shy, suspicious Indians who passed our doorway.

Our first assignment was a difficult one. The people were quite unfriendly, and some were fanatical in their bitter opposition to our presence in their city. On occasion small crowds would gather to hurl insults, punctuated by stones, both large and small. Now and then school children would parade in the dusty street before our home and repeat what they had been taught to say against us. The Indians from the countryside were especially timid about having any friendly contact with us because of intimidation by some of the townspeople. As a result it was often difficult to get the bare necessities of life—fruits and vegetables, or charcoal for the kitchen stove.

Added to these physical factors was an inward sense of human loneliness. There was never fear, but one was aware that there were very few who in the remotest sense were the least friendly.

One noon as we were eating we heard a rattling on the gate as though someone were asking for admission. I excused myself from the table and went to the porch. Then I saw an Indian woman standing outside the gate. Quickly I went down to inquire what she might want. She was no one I had ever seen before, and the small bundle she carried on her shoulder did not indicate that she had any vegetables to offer for sale.

Pointing to a gospel verse we had put on the porch she inquired, "Are you the people who have come to tell us about the living God?"

Her question startled me. No one had ever made that query before. Therefore, with surprise, I answered, "*Mamita*, yes we are."

Then she raised her hand inside the locked gate and began to pray. I can still see that hand and arm with its beads, in typical Indian style. She wore the heavy hat of the mountain women, the white homespun waist with its primitive embroidery, and her dress was *balleta* (coarse woolen cloth) with a brightly colored homemade belt. Of course, she was barefooted.

She prayed for the blessing of God upon the inhabitants of this home. She asked that we have courage for the service committed to us, that we have joy in doing God's bidding, and she prayed that many would hear and obey the words of the gospel. Then she pronounced a blessing from God upon me.

The prayer concluded, she withdrew her hand. Then she smiled at me through the gate with a final, *Dios le bendiga*, "God bless you." Her eyes fairly shone as she spoke those words, and then she bowed and turned to her left.

I was so astonished by all of this that for part of a minute I stood speechless and motionless. Quickly I remembered that it was the heat of the day, and that she should come in and eat with us. In a matter of seconds I had unlocked the gate and stepped out to call her back. She could not have gone more than five or ten yards.

But she was not there! It was at least fifty yards from our gate to the corner of the street, and there was no gate along that stretch of wall, either on our side of the street or across the way.

I ran to the corner with the persuasion that if it had been possible for her to have reached that far then certainly she would be right there. Immediately I looked to the right but she was not there. As I ran to the corner I could look down our street for nearly half a mile, and there were no openings in the wall in that direction.

The closest gate was to my right and that was nearly a block away. There I ran. I rushed inside the open gate and there were my two closest neighbors. Hastily I inquired, "Did an Indian woman just come in here?"

"No, sir, we have been right here in the gate for an hour or more, and nobody has entered or left during that time."

I thanked them, and hastened back to the corner. There was not a soul in sight. I waited there for more than ten minutes, but no one appeared on the street. Slowly I retraced my steps to my own gate, and after locking it again went back to the table.

"Where have you been so long?" inquired my wife.

"There was an elderly Indian woman knocking on the gate. She prayed for us and invoked God's blessing upon us and then started on down the street. I unlocked the gate and stepped out to call her, but she was not along the wall as I had expected. So

I ran to the corner and sought her, but in vain."

"Strange!"

We spoke no more about the matter. However, for days afterward my heart remained strangely moved. It burned within me as I recalled the Indian woman's prayer, and it was strengthened by the blessing she had pronounced upon me. There seemed to be an aroma indescribably sweet and indefinable which certainly did not come from the flowers in the garden.

After some days, I began to reflect upon that word in Hebrews 13:2, "Be not forgetful to entertain strangers: for thereby some have entertained angels unawares" (KJV). I began to understand that the Almighty had none of His earthly servants at hand to encourage two young missionaries, so He was pleased to send an angel from heaven.

V. Raymond Edman was a missionary to Ecuador and past president of Wheaton College.

As Tall as Trees

by Marilynn Carlson Webber and
William D. Webber

A couple of years ago, Tina Lee's husband, David, was clearing some land to enlarge their produce garden near their home in rural Georgia. The Lees enjoy gardening, and their crops of peas, butterbeans, tomatoes, and potatoes (among other things) fed them year 'round. As David drove the tractor, Tina went inside to answer the telephone, which was by a window from which she could watch both her husband and their two-year-old son Joshua, who was playing near the house.

As she picked up the phone, she was horrified to look outside and see David on the ground—and the tractor on top of him.

"Joshua, stay right there!" she yelled to her son as she raced past him to try to save her husband.

Tina arrived to find the tractor pinning David—by the rubber sole of his work boot. The ignition key was turned halfway to off, which had stalled the large tractor. Tina immediately climbed up and turned off the motor, then she helped David out from under the tractor, and together they were able to right it. The worst injury he suffered was a twisted ankle.

As they discussed the accident, David shook his head and

said he didn't understand what had happened: He remembered the tractor's being right over him—then moving away from him as if someone had shoved it aside. He also had no idea why the engine had stalled when it did. He had expected to lose his leg if not his life.

Just then little Joshua came running over to his parents.

"Did you see him, Daddy?" Joshua asked.

"Who?"

"The man," the little boy said, his eyes still wide. "He was as tall as the trees! He moved the tractor when it was falling on Daddy, then he turned the key."

Tina and David hadn't seen, but they both knew that "from the mouths of babes" had come the only explanation for what had happened. "I've always believed in angels and felt their comfort," says Tina, "but this solidified my belief that angels are always protecting us, too!"

Marilynn is one of the world's leading authorities on angels, and a featured speaker at churches, conventions, and women's groups; William has served as both pastor and seminary professor.

A Prisoner... and Yet

by Corrie ten Boom

Together we entered the terrifying building. At a table were women who took away all our possessions. Everyone had to undress completely and then go to a room where her hair was checked. If anyone had lice, her hair was clipped short....

I asked a woman who was busy checking the possessions of the new arrivals if I might use the toilet. She pointed to a door, and I discovered that the convenience was nothing more than a hole in the shower-room floor. Betsie stayed beside me all the time. Suddenly I had an inspiration: "Quick, take off your woolen underwear," I whispered to her. I rolled it up with mine and laid the bundle in the corner with my little Bible. The spot was alive with cockroaches, but I didn't worry about that. I felt wonderfully relieved and happy. "The Lord is busy answering our prayers, Betsie," I whispered. "We shall not have to make the sacrifice of all our clothes."

We hurried back to the row of women waiting to be undressed. A little later, after we had had our showers and put on our shirts and shabby dresses, I hid the roll of underwear and my Bible under my dress. It did bulge out obviously through my dress; but I prayed, "Lord, cause now thine angels to surround me; and let them not be transparent today, for the guards must not see me." I felt perfectly at ease. Calmly, I passed the guards. Everyone was checked, from the front, the sides, the back. Not a bulge escaped the eyes of the guard. The woman just in front of me had hidden a woolen vest under her dress; it was taken from her. They let me pass, for they did not see me. Betsie, right behind me, was searched.

But outside awaited another danger. On each side of the door were women who looked everyone over for a second time. They felt over the body of each one who passed. I knew they would not see me, for the angels were still surrounding me. I was not even surprised when they passed me by; but within me rose the jubilant cry, "O Lord, if Thou dost so answer prayer, I can face even Ravensbruck unafraid."

Corrie ten Boom was a world renowned author and speaker, and survivor of Nazi concentration camps.

Two Came for Katherine

Mike Lambly, retold by Gary Kinnaman

Katherine was born weighing all of one pound, nine ounces and was quickly rushed off to the neonatal unit. She looked perfect—every little finger and toe was there, just in miniature. We were so happy she was alive. And there was hope—hope for a miracle.

The cards and flowers and congratulations came, the loving letters and notes of encouragement and prayer. And every day Katherine lived was a miracle. Three days. Then five. Then seven. The doctors were amazed!

A week after the birth, I decided to go see Katherine during the day between my sales calls. As I walked the hospital halls to the neonatal unit, I thought of my tiny baby and the long fight that was ahead of her. I reached the special care unit and pulled on the required gown. Pushing up my sleeves to perform the obligatory fingers-to-elbow scrubbing, I turned to look through the large glass window to see Katherine lying in her incubator and glanced around at some of the other babies.

I looked back toward Katherine as I kept scrubbing. Suddenly I stopped motionless over the basin, transfixed at the sight of two very large figures standing on either side of her incubator. They had to be at least ten feet tall, with very large shoulders. And they shone with the brightest white light I have ever seen. I could see no face to determine if the beings were male or female, but as I stared I knew they were angels and I was certain they were there to protect my daughter. The length of their appearance was very brief, and yet it seemed as if time stood still forever.

I walked over to the incubator and saw Katherine lying there peacefully with her little cap on to keep her warm. I told her that all would be well and that not only did Jesus love her, but that she had angels watching over her and protecting her. I couldn't wait to share the news with my wife Jeanne that the Lord had sent two angels to watch over and protect our baby. And that everything was going to be fine.

But by the next day, Katherine was gone. We had a wonderfully peaceful memorial service, but in the days that followed, I began to question the Lord: "Why did you send those angels? I thought they were there to protect my daughter, to keep her safe as she grew."

I'm sure it was no coincidence that Jeanne and I just happened to watch Billy Graham on television about two weeks later. His subject: angels. The believer, he declared, is never out of the Lord's care. Even at our death, he provides angels to usher us into his presence. Yes, the angels that visited Katherine's incubator had a mission, but it was not just to protect her. More importantly, they came to take her to Jesus.

Miracles for

EVERYDAY

LIFE

It is possible that you are missing the greatest miracle

that God's sovereign hand is moving through every

single event of your life

whether the moment is exalted and exhilarating

or tempestuous and traumatic.

Robert L. Wise

Miracles for EVERYDAY LIFE

Everyday miracles. It sounds like an oxymoron. Most of us think of miracles as *big* things. Attention-catching, awe-inspiring events. It seems ridiculous—almost sacrilegious—to lump them together with everyday events. Yet the question presents itself: does God perform miracles in the ordinary experiences of life?

If the answer is yes (and it probably is), we risk losing sight of the fact that miracles are, in fact, special, unexplainable, and, well...*miraculous*. Yet, if we stretch our minds enough to include this new and broader picture, we may also come closer to accepting the possibility that God still performs them today.

While we don't want to trivialize God's actions, it may be helpful to look at the stories in this section—as well as full-scale biblical miracles—and say, "This could happen to me, too. Maybe it already has, and I didn't even recognize it."

God's miracles are for everybody. Not all of them are performed for those we see as "super-saints," in order to create a huge, dramatic effect. In God's eyes, every person has value beyond measure.

In our world, every miracle does as well.

INCREDIBLE

by David Jeremiah

I t happened around noon on Mother's Day. According to a
national news report, twenty-seven-year-old Michael Murray
decided to take his two children to the medical center in
Massachusetts where their mother was on duty as a surgical
nurse. The family wanted to drop off some Mother's Day presents: a gold necklace with the words "Number 1 Mom," and a
single rose. With their mission accomplished, the father and
his two children made their way back to the darkened indoor
garage where the car had been parked.

Murray gently set the infant seat and three-month-old
Matthew on the sun roof of the car and turned his attention to
buckling Matthew's twenty-month-old sister into her seat.
Without thinking further, Murray slid into the driver's seat and
drove off, forgetting that Matthew was still on the roof.

Moving slowly from the darkened garage into the bright
sunlight, Murray drove through busy streets toward Interstate
290. Despite heavy traffic, nobody beeped or waved to warn
him that anything was wrong. Pulling onto the expressway that
cuts through the city, the driver accelerated to 50 mph and
then he heard it—a scraping on the roof of his car as the tiny
seat with Matthew strapped in began to slide. He said, "I

looked to where Matthew should have been in the car, and then in the rearview mirror I saw him sliding down the highway in his infant seat. "That's where he landed. In the middle of the interstate, in the path of oncoming traffic."

The car seat flew off the roof and hit the road and was sliding down the highway almost as fast as the cars were coming toward it. An antique dealer named James Boothby was following the Murray car when he saw the whole event unfold. He saw young Matthew sail off the roof and hit the road.

He said:

I saw something in the air. At first I thought someone had thrown some garbage out the window. Then I saw it and thought it was a doll. Then the doll opened its mouth and I realized this was a little baby. It just landed on the road. It bounced a couple of times, and it never tipped over. It just landed on the road and slid along a bit. I slammed on my brakes and turned my car around in the lane so that no other cars could go by. I jumped from the car, and I ran and found an uninjured baby in an undamaged car seat, and scooped him up in my arms and took him back and gave him to his petrified father.

That true story has to be as close to a grade A miracle as anything you and I have ever experienced. God intervened in that situation or it would have been an incredible tragedy.

David Jeremiah is senior pastor of Shadow Mountain Community Church in San Diego, president of Christian Heritage College, founder and host of "Turning Point" radio program, and author of many books including What the Bible Says about Angels.

A SHIELD OF PROTECTION

by Pat Robertson

Back in 1977, unusual weather conditions threatened to destroy the orange groves in Norvell Hayes's part of Florida. The trees in the area were covered with icicles, and the orange growers knew from past experience that it was highly likely that the cold would kill their crops.

But Norvell wasn't willing to accept the disaster that seemed inevitable. He believed God could save his trees, and he asked for a miracle.

"I got in my car, drove to the orange grove, and parked along the highway," he said. "I just looked at the grove and told the devil to take his hands off the orange trees. Then I asked the Father, in Jesus' name, to let His power come and hover around my fruit trees and not let them die."

A few weeks later, the sun began to shine again and things warmed up. Norvell still gets excited when he describes the result of his prayer. "Fruit was developing on my trees! The twenty-five hundred orange trees on the property across the road, which was owned by another grower, were dead. But on my side of the road, it was different. It was as though a shield had been placed on my property line, which stopped the potentially damaging frost from crossing it. I didn't lose a tree."

Pat Robertson is a Christian statesman and founder of the Christian Broadcasting Network, the 700 Club, Regent University, and the Christian Coalition.

DON'T *EVER* LET YOUR GUARD DOWN

by Donald Jacobson

I was having a wonderful time. I was standing alone at the edge of Rosalyn Lake in sparsely settled country about twenty miles east of Portland, Oregon. Late-afternoon sunlight gilded the calm water. The air was chill—it was late November. Behind me Big Boy, my black Labrador retriever, fidgeted and whined. He was waiting for a pair of circling mallards to come within range. So was I.

I clicked off the safety on my 12-gauge, double-barreled shotgun, feeling the excitement that every hunter knows. I was twenty-four-years-old, happily married, I had a good job in the construction business. I loved the outdoors. I was completely happy doing what I was doing. And I was about five seconds away from sudden death.

My decision to go hunting had been an impulsive one. A new stock had been put on my gun; I wanted to try it out. So I stuffed a few shells in my jeans, whistled to Big Boy, jumped in my car, and took off for the lake. I had never hunted it, but I figured some ducks might be there. I didn't tell my wife Brenda or anyone else where I was going (mistake number one); I figured I would be back in time for supper. Our friends Jeri and

Eric Weber were coming over around eight.

Behind me Big Boy whined louder and plunged around, in and out of the water. Eagerness is a fine trait in a gundog, but a retriever has to learn to stay as still as a statue until he gets the order to retrieve. Ducks can spot any movement—and when they do, they're gone. I spoke urgently in a harsh whisper to Big Boy, but he didn't obey. I would have cuffed him with my hand, but he was just out of reach. I kept my eye on the ducks, sure they would be spooked by the dog. Big Boy kept moving until, exasperated, I did a very foolish thing. I shifted the gun to my right hand (mistake number two). Holding it by the barrels, I made an angry sweep behind me, hoping to freeze Big Boy into immobility.

What happened next was so swift and shocking that I still can hardly believe it. Probably the screw in the new stock somehow came loose and allowed the trigger guard to depress the trigger. In any case, a stunning burst of sound shattered the quietness of the lake. Something like a gigantic fist slammed into my body just above my right hip. I was hurled into the water. Even as I fell, the unthinkable flashed across my mind in letters of fire: "I've shot myself!"

My first reaction was numbness and total shock. The water was not deep, 10 inches perhaps. I tried to fire the three-shot SOS distress signal that hunters use in emergencies, but my slowness of reloading my two-shot gun made my signals ineffective. I tried to stand up, but my right leg was paralyzed. I dragged myself out of the water. Again I tried to stand. Again I failed. I would not believe that this had happened to me, an experienced hunter, a firearms safety fanatic.

A 12-gauge shotgun is a deadly weapon of enormous power. A single shell loaded with Number Four shot—a heavy duck load—contains about 150 lead pellets. At 40 or 50 yards they expand into a pattern eight or ten feet across, but at very close range they are condensed into an almost solid projection that will tear a hole the size of a doorknob in almost anything. Such a hole was now blasted into my right side.

I tried to crawl away from the lake, but could manage only a few feet at a time. Then the pain began. Unbelievable pain. Later I learned that one pellet was carried by my bloodstream completely through the chambers of my heart and into one of my lungs. I was in such agony that I became nauseated. Then I couldn't breathe. At that point I said, "Lord, if You're going to take me home, please do it quickly. Or else help me with this pain." The moment I said that, the pain lessened. I knew then that I had a chance of surviving because the Lord was right there, listening to me.

All my life I've felt close to the Lord. My parents are missionaries far up in the northern part of Canada. They believe in miracles, and they taught us children to believe in them, too. I didn't know it then, but one extraordinary miracle had already taken place: incredibly, the charge of shot had not gone all the way through my body. It had stopped inside, tearing away muscles, nicking one kidney, damaging the liver—but missing the spine. If one pellet had gone all the way through, I would have bled to death.

Somehow I kept crawling until I came to a tree. Big Boy stayed with me, puzzled and troubled. Anxious now to please, he brought a stick for me to throw. This frightened me because he could be very rough and insistent whenever we played fetch. "Lord," I murmured, "I can't handle this." And for the first time in his life Big Boy broke off the game before it had even started and lay down quietly beside me.

I lay huddled under the tree, watching the light fade out of the sky. A pale moon began to glow above the lake; the temperature was dropping. My wet clothing offered little protection. Soon, I knew, people would be looking for me. I wondered if the moonlight would help them. I thought of Brenda, and how much I loved her. I figured I could hang on until morning. With the Lord's help—and maybe Big Boy's warmth.

Meantime, back at our house, Brenda was puzzled when I didn't appear for supper. By the time the Webers arrived, she was starting to worry. She telephoned her father, John Van Diest, who at that time was publisher of the Multnomah Press in Portland. A close friend and working companion in the construction business, Blair Andersen, arrived. By ten o'clock they were all out looking. They checked places where they knew I sometimes hunted. Nothing. A fog began rolling in, blotting out the moonlight. Everyone was doing a lot of praying.

Despite her fears, Brenda remained very steady, very calm. When you ask the Lord to supply your needs, He does. About midnight, Brenda's father called from the area where he was searching and suggested she search the Rosalyn Lake area, although he warned it was an unlikely place for me to hunt. She took off in one of the cars with Jeri and Eric, but now the fog was so dense that they lost a lot of time because visibility was down to about 15 feet. It was about 2:11 A.M. when they found themselves creeping along one of the roads near the lake. Suddenly Eric braked to a stop. "Thought I saw something glimmer," he said. Sure enough, it was my car. Everything intact.

Eric shouted my name at the top of his lungs. Then he listened. "There!" he said to the girls. "Did you hear that?" They had heard nothing. Again he shouted. Again the girls heard nothing, but Eric's sharp ears caught a faint, far-off sound. It was my feeble voice, trying to answer him. Incredibly, I was still conscious.

By now the temperature was down to thirty-three degrees. My voice was weak from thirst and loss of blood. I had tried to suck water from my soaked parka all night, but my throat was almost too dry for me to speak. So I tried to whistle. A few moments later Eric came plunging through the woods and found me.

They couldn't move me; I'm six feet three, and heavy. They had to find a farmhouse, wake up the people, and ask them to call the volunteer fire department in the little town of Sandy. Those guys were magnificent. In a little while there were about six vehicles, including police and ambulance, standing by with all sorts of emergency equipment. They tried to give me an IV, but I'd lost so much blood they couldn't find a vein. My body temperature was down to ninety-four degrees. Doctors said later that in one more hour I would have been dead from exposure.

My rescuers carried me out of the woods. Then they radioed for a rescue helicopter. Amazingly, the pilot found a hole in the fog and landed near us there in Sandy. They flew to Gresham Hospital where, again amazingly, the fog thinned enough for them to land. The minute they landed, it closed again. They were stuck there for several hours.

A medical team was waiting. By 7:00 A.M. I was in surgery. The doctors worked for almost three hours, repairing torn tissues. They removed dozens of lead pellets, but they had to leave a lot of them in. Then the surgeon came out and told Brenda and her parents that I had made it through the operation. For the first time, Brenda broke down and cried.

The doctors were afraid of gangrene; all the conditions for it were present. But thanks to their skill and the Lord's protection, it never developed. I was in three different hospitals for a total of one month, but before long, I was as good as ever.

I almost lost my life that afternoon, but I gained two things that are going to stay with me for the rest of my days. The first—and this is a message for outdoorsmen and hunters everywhere—is this: don't *ever* think you're immune to trouble, don't *ever* let your guard down, don't *ever* forget the dangers involved in what you're doing. In a way, the more experienced you are, the more risk there may be, because you get overconfident and then you get careless—as I did—just for a split second. That split second can cost you your life, or the life of another hunter. No matter how confident you are, you can never be sure.

Likewise—and I think this is the most important thing I have to pass on—you can never be sure about how much time you may have left in this life, either. Standing there on the shore of Rosalyn Lake I was just twenty-four years old—strong, healthy, confident, brimming with life and vitality. The next instant I was staring straight into the blank eyes of death.

If you think that there is time left to get your spiritual life in order, then think again. The time to make a decision about that is now. What if you never have another chance?

Don Jacobson is President, Multnomah Publishers, Inc.

PLEASE LORD, LET HER LIVE

by Kenneth Taylor

K enneth Taylor's family was living in the small town of Winona Lake, located 120 miles from Chicago. Kenneth worked in Chicago and commuted home on the weekends. His wife, Margaret, was pregnant with their fifth child.

I received the call around 2:00 A.M. Fortunately, the ancient car started on that frigid January morning, and I arrived at the hospital about three hours later. It was a country hospital without the usual "no fathers permitted" rules of that period. When I arrived in the delivery room, Margaret was under heavy sedation. Almost immediately I saw the top of our baby's head begin to appear, but one of the nurses pushed it back and held it there while they waited for the doctor to arrive.

I had never seen a birth and knew very little about the process, but it seemed to me it would be safer to let my little one be born. The nurses said no, they had to wait until the doctor was present. When he hadn't arrived after fifteen minutes, I demanded that they let the baby out, but they still refused. The nurses were obviously much afraid of the doctor, who was also the owner of the hospital, but finally one of them hesitantly called him again and found he had gone back to sleep.

After another fifteen minutes he arrived, very grouchy and surly. Ignoring me, he walked over to Margaret and pushed roughly on her abdomen, and our baby girl popped out— white and silent. The nurses slapped her to try to get her to breathe, but nothing happened. I remember how panicky one of the nurses was.

"Get the oxygen! Get the oxygen!" she exclaimed.

"Fool!" the doctor snarled. "If it isn't breathing, what good would oxygen do?"

At this point I went into a side room and got down on my knees and prayed, "Lord, if this child is ever going to need you in her entire life, it is right now. Please let her live. Still, Lord, if for some reason—perhaps because of something in her life you don't want her to have to face, or if perhaps she would not receive the grace of Christ or would abandon Him—then your will be done. It would be better to take her now. But please, Lord, let her live."

I hurried back to the delivery room, and just then the baby began to breathe and to cry. A few moments later I went back to the little "prayer room" to thank the Lord for His kindness. And so baby Janet came into our lives as a special act of God.

Kenneth Taylor is founder and chairman of the board for Tyndale House Publishers, Inc., and is best known for his paraphrase, The Living Bible.

STOP THE RAIN, LORD

by Adrian Rogers

We were in Moscow, Russia during the Orthodox Easter. An elaborate sound stage had been constructed in Red Square by Campus Crusade for Christ. There was to be a concert and then a gospel presentation. Many thousands had gathered, and the service was to be telecast throughout all Russia.

I was with Dr. Bill Bright, founder of Campus Crusade, in prayer when a messenger came with the news, "It's raining. Because the power lines are down everywhere, the government officials say that we must shut down the event."

"We can't do that. Too much money, time, and faith have been invested," Bill Bright said. The leadership of our event pleaded with the officials for just ten minutes more to give the rain time to stop. It looked impossible. Gray clouds covered the sky over the Kremlin. The cold rain fell on our heads.

A group of prayer warriors huddled under a scaffold and began to sing and pray. I can hear them now and see them in my memory as they looked up into the face of those threatening clouds and called out, "Stop the rain, Lord, stop the rain."

I testify to you that in nine and a half minutes an amazing thing happened. It seemed as if a giant squeegee were drawn across the sky. A blazing sun began to smile from an azure sky. Our God had answered prayer.

Adrian Rogers is the pastor of a 28,000-member church in Memphis, Tennessee; three-time president of Southern Baptist Convention; founder of "Love Worth Finding," a TV and radio ministry; and author of many books including Believe in Miracles but Trust in Jesus.

An Unseen Hand to Guide the Course

by Sara Boyd

Dense fog crept across the dawn, draping a gray shroud over Chesapeake Bay. The two Boyd brothers, David and Jim, had been looking forward to this day for quite a while. They didn't often get the chance to go fishing in the bay together, and unexpected weather now threatened their careful plans. Even as they made the last minute preparations that morning, they considered canceling the trip. However, since both were licensed sea captains, well trained in blind navigation, and since the boat was outfitted with the necessary instruments, they decided to give it a go. Mere fog would not deny their sharing each other's company on the open sea this day.

Keeping their voices hushed in the early morning, David and Jim started for the marina. It wasn't long before they uncovered the one fatal flaw in their plans: every bait shop in town was closed for the holiday. They needed live clams to catch the tautog (small fish with teeth much like a five-year-old child's) swimming near the remains of an old shipwreck at the entrance to the bay. The weather hadn't dampened their mood, and neither would the missing clams. To get that rare time together, they happily settled for frozen crab taken from the freezer at home.

David, a marine biologist, and Jim, a lawyer, passed a few hours in conversation before they realized that the tautog had discerning taste—they wouldn't be tempted by old bait not to their liking. Eventually, David and Jim decided to give in and head for home.

Visibility dropped to thirty feet as fog continued to fill the bay. Buoys marked the shipping channel that led into Hampton Roads; David kept his eyes on a navigational chart that indicated their location.

Just as the boat came close enough to one of the buoys for Jim to see its dim outline, David took his hand off the tiller for just a moment to check a position on his chart. The boat swung off course and circled back into the fog. As quickly as he could, David grabbed the tiller again and, using the instruments, determined that the boat had made a complete circle and was back to the exact same direction in which it had been headed.

He glanced at Jim and saw his brother staring hard at something just at the edge of visibility.

"What are you trying to see in this pea soup?" he asked jokingly.

"There's something odd—" Jim's eyes opened wide as he broke off. "David! Two men are clinging to that buoy!"

"What?! There can't be. Maybe you're—"

"No, I'm not seeing things," Jim interjected. "*Look* over there."

And then David saw them as well. Two men, weather-beaten and obviously exhausted, slumped against the buoy. The two brothers moved in for the rescue.

Later, the men told their story. Ben Matthews was visiting from another state. His long-time friend, Sam Hansen, lived in one of the towns near the bay. The two men decided to go fishing before Ben returned home. They started out on the afternoon of December 31 in a small rented rowboat. The rowboat was equipped with a tiny motor, but only later did they realize it did not have two of the most important features—a radio, and a compass. They were still out on the water when the fog starting rolling in, slowly it seemed. However, it wasn't long before they had no idea which way to turn; the fog quickly erased every point of reference that could be seen from out on the water.

They went in circles, with no way to find direction, and soon the engine ran low on fuel. Sam shut off the motor as they tried to figure out what to do next. Through the blanket of silence came the distinctive, resonating *bong* of an ocean bell buoy, indicating that there was a channel nearby. The two were relieved, knowing that other ships would have to pass in order to get into the harbor. They started the motor and made straight for that sound. The buoy appeared out of the mist, and they tied their little boat to it. Ben, hoping the buoy would be a better vantage point, climbed onto it and tried in vain to spot any passing ship. His eyes strained to make out even a sketchy outline in the gray vapor, but there was nothing. Sam scrambled up after him, and together they kept their eyes peeled for any sign of rescue.

Through the long night they stayed there, tossed to and fro with the buoy as it continued to broadcast its message through the darkness: *bong, bong, bong*. Two or three times Sam and Ben heard the Virginia pilot boat pass by, out to sea and then back in again, to escort ocean vessels into the harbor. But it was never close enough to be seen through the fog. The pilot boat navigated by radar, so it did not need to pass close by the buoy markers. And certainly no one aboard it would be looking for two men sitting out there in the middle of the shipping channel!

In desperation, Ben and Sam dragged what they could from the boat, intending to start a fire that would serve both as a beacon and for warmth—it was so cold out there! As flames from the burning tackle boxes and life preservers flared, toxic smoke formed and hung in thick black clouds around them. The fumes were unbearable, even if there was some warmth from the fire. It was a dismal failure.

By the time dawn came, Ben and Sam were weary from gripping the bouncing float, exhausted from stress, and starting to suffer from exposure. Then, they heard the most defeating sound yet—the line that secured the rowboat to the marker snapped, and together they watched the small craft get carried away. *Now* they knew the true meaning of isolation. In addition, Ben was diabetic, and his body began to suffer in still other ways as the effects of the long ordeal settled further into their bodies, their minds, and their spirits. Four more hours passed, and the men sunk further into the hopelessness of their situation.

God, please, Ben pleaded, *You have to help us. We can't hang on much longer. I don't want to slip into the sea and never be seen again.*

Suddenly, as if by miracle answer, a boat appeared in the fog. It was heading directly toward them. Spirits soared and the two friends felt a flash of renewed energy as they prepared to start signaling those on board.

Just as suddenly, the boat was gone, disappearing back into the fog. Anguish wrapped deadly hands around their spirits and wrung them dry of the little hope that remained. Each felt a heavy weight drop inside himself as the only help they'd had in sixteen hours simply vanished before their eyes.

David and Jim believe that God is in His heaven, that He knows the situations of men. They believe He spun the boat in a full circle and returned it to the buoy's locale. This second time, the two brothers saw the stranded men at the end of their endurance.

There is a popular gospel song that says, "His eye is on the sparrow, and I know He watches me." That day, Ben and Sam knew the miraculous care of the God who watches over them. His care is often in the unspectacular details: David and Jim were expert boatmen. They decided to go fishing in spite of bad weather. They just happened to come into the shipping channel by that particular marker. And then there's the boat, miraculously completing its circle to end up pointing exactly the same direction it had been before David took his hand off the tiller—as if another hand, so often unseen, gently and powerfully guided its course.

Sara Boyd serves on various philanthropic boards, is Master Docere of the Chrysler Museum, and president of the Virginia Lawyers' Wives Association.

A DIVE OF FAITH

by James Dobson

I have no doubts that miracles occur every day.... I have been privileged to witness some incredible evidences of God's power in my life and in the experience of those with whom I am close. One of the most miraculous events happened to my friend, Jim Davis, when he and his family visited Yellowstone National Park in 1970. Jim was a guest on the *Focus on the Family* broadcast some time later, and he shared that experience with our listeners. These are his approximate words on that occasion:

> My wife and I were both raised in Christian families, and we were taught the power of prayer. But we were not living very godly lives. We did not pray together or have a family altar in our home. About that time, she made a wonderful commitment to the Lord and began praying for me. She bought me a research Bible, and I began to get into the Word. Things started to change in my heart, but I still wasn't mature spiritually.
>
> That summer, we went on a vacation to Yellowstone Park with four other couples. Several of these friends went fishing

the next day in an aluminum boat, and one of the ladies hooked a trout. She leaned over to net the fish, and her glasses fell off. They immediately sank to the bottom of the lake. She was very disturbed by the loss because it was the beginning of their vacation, and she could not drive or read without the glasses. She also got severe headaches when she didn't wear them.

That night, everyone was talking about the glasses and how unfortunate it was that they were lost. Then my wife said, "No sweat. Jim is a great scuba diver. He'll go out and find them for you."

"Hey, thanks a lot," I said. "Do you know that Yellowstone Lake has 172 miles of shoreline, and every tree is coniferous and looks exactly the same? There's no way I can get a fix on where you guys were when the glasses went overboard. Besides, the water is very, very cold—fifty degrees. They won't even allow you to water-ski out there. And I don't have a wet suit—just a pair of fins and a snorkel."

My objections fell on deaf ears. She told me privately that she intended to pray that the Lord would help me find those glasses.

Yeah, sure, I thought.

The next morning we got in the boat and headed about a half mile out from the shore.

"Uh, where do you think you dropped them?" I asked.

"It seems like about here," someone said.

Well, I got in the water, and it was freezing. I took hold of a rope, and the boat dragged me along the surface as I looked at the bottom. The water was about ten feet deep and crystal clear. We made a swath about fifty feet long and then turned and worked our way back. After about twenty minutes of this search, I was just chilled to the bone. I prayed a little prayer *and said, Lord, if You know where those glasses are, I sure wish You'd tell me. I wasn't convinced He knew. It's a very big lake.*

But a little voice in my mind said, I know exactly where they are. Get in the boat, and I'll take you to them. Well, I didn't tell anyone about this message because I was too embarrassed to say it. But about twenty minutes later I was just shivering, and I said, Lord, if You still know where those glasses are, I'll get in the boat.

I called out to my friends and said, "We're in the wrong place. They're over there."

I got in the boat and pointed to a spot I thought the Lord was telling me about. The driver said, "No, we weren't that far out." But we kept going, and I said, "Stop. Right here. This is the place."

I jumped in the water and looked down. We were right on top of those glasses. I dove to the bottom and came up with the prize. It was one of the clearest answers to prayer I've ever experienced, and it set me on fire spiritually. It was also an incredible witness to my wife and all my friends. And I'll never forget those sparkling glasses at the bottom of Yellowstone Lake.

As dramatic as this story is, I can personally vouch for its authenticity as Jim told it. There are many witnesses who remember that remarkable day on Yellowstone Lake.

James Dobson is the founder and president of Focus on the Family Ministries and author of numerous best-selling books includ-ing When God Doesn't Make Sense.

A Dead End

by Ron Mehl

For two frightened, hurting, young men, it looked very much like a dead end.

Neither thought he could go much further. Neither knew what to do. Both realized—without admitting it out loud—that they might not live through the night.

Jonah, a high-school graduate from our church, was badly wounded. He had a severe concussion, and his arm was shattered with a grisly compound fracture—jagged bone piercing the skin. Both ankles were injured: the right one fractured, the left with torn ligaments. The temperature on the side of the mountain was dropping rapidly, and their light clothing was soaked clear through.

But worst of all was the darkness. A tranquil sea of stars burning silently overhead only seemed to mock their predicament. They needed better illumination than pale starlight to scale the seventy-degree incline of an icy mountainside! One false step might send them plunging into the darkness below. Again.

They had to decide. To go further seemed foolish—perhaps deadly. But staying where they were was no solution at all.

Jonah needed medical help—fast. And dressed the way they were, they would die of exposure. Which was preferable...a quick death or a slow one? Billy didn't know what to do, and Jonah was so badly injured he could hardly speak for himself. It was on Billy's shoulders—a heavy load for an eighteen-year-old. *What should he do? Which way should he turn?*

"I—I don't think we're going to make it," Billy told Jonah, shivering. "I don't think we can go any further. We can't see. It's just too dark."

If they could see, they had at least a slim chance of getting out alive. But without light—well, it didn't seem much use. Then Billy saw something that made no sense. A soft glow seemed to be radiating out of Jonah's midsection.

"What's that?"

Terror had fallen suddenly on that bright Sunday afternoon, near the end of the last leg of the boys' last summer outing.

Earlier in the day, the six high-school buddies had set out to conquer the 10,495-foot summit of Mount Jefferson in the Oregon Cascades. Besides Jonah and Billy, the climbing party included Chris, Dan, Jake, and Ben. Eric, not feeling well, had decided to remain at base camp. All of the boys were eighteen, except for Ben, who was still seventeen.

Just weeks before, the inseparable friends had graduated from Aloha High School in Beaverton, Oregon. Each had set his sights on a different college. But they all wanted one last glorious adventure—together—before they went their separate ways.

When you're eighteen, you look ahead and see open doors and green lights and wide highways stretching off into the hazy distance of the future.

When you're eighteen, climbing mountain peaks looks like the easy and natural thing to do.

When you're eighteen, you never think about the possibility of running into a dead end.

A little after three o'clock on that July afternoon, the boys were about four hundred feet from the summit. Just four hundred more steps through rock and snow and they would stand together at that dazzling pinnacle. From the top they would be able to look north and see Mount Hood, Mount Adams, Mount St. Helens, and Mount Rainier. To the south they could count on seeing the Three Sisters towering nearby, the skiers' favorite—Mount Bachelor—and perhaps even Mount Shasta, shimmering on the southern horizon.

But it wasn't to be. Not on this trip. Not on this day. As he glanced up at the summit looming just ahead of him, Chris accidentally dislodged a large rock that went crashing down the mountain. Chris yelled a warning, and Jonah, ten yards below, leaped out of the way—and lost his balance.

Jonah tumbled down the steep incline followed by the rolling boulder. Three-quarters of the way down the slope, the rock grazed Jonah's head and knocked him unconscious.

"No!" Chris yelled. "I killed my friend! *I killed Jonah!*" Then Chris too was sliding down the snowy slope after his friend.

As it turned out, he had quite a ways to go. Jonah fell more than nine hundred feet.

In the fading light of late afternoon, he lay in a crumpled heap at the bottom of a deep ravine creasing the side of the mountain. Logically, no one could have survived such a fall. After all, people die from falls off bicycles, falls down a few concrete stairs, or falls from the top of step ladders. A fall of nine feet can kill you. A fall of ninety feet is nearly always fatal. *How could anyone fall nine hundred feet and live?*

Chris stopped his own slide just inches from the edge of the crevasse where his friend was lying. As he clambered down the shaley slope, he thought—just for a moment—that he'd heard the sweetest sound imaginable. But it couldn't be...could it? *Yes!* Jonah had moaned! *He was alive!* His left arm had snapped like a match stick, and his face was a mask of blood. But he was alive!

Slowly the others picked their way toward the ravine, white faced, wide eyed. After a quick huddle Chris and Jake were dispatched back to the trailhead to find help. Ben, Dan, and Billy would wait with Jonah.

But what would they *do* with Jonah? Everyone could feel the temperature drop as the sun slipped lower on the horizon. That's the way it is at those elevations. No matter how warm the day, the darkness brings winter. The boy's light summer attire—shorts and fleece pullovers—wouldn't be much help when the mercury plunged below freezing.

Slowly, painfully, they began to move toward the safety of camp. Ben and Dan decided to hurry on ahead, planning to return to meet Billy and Jonah with warm clothes and food.

Jonah could hardly walk. There were stretches on that terrible climb back up the steep slope where Billy had to get behind Jonah, put the top of his head on Jonah's backside, and use his wrestler's strength to push him up the incline.

Most of the time it was just step after agonizing step, swinging ice axes and pulling themselves up inch by inch, foot by foot.

Then Jonah's ax missed contact, and he fell.

Grabbing hold of each other, the boys slid down a long

snowfield—straight toward the churning waters of Milk Creek below. As he was sliding, Billy thought he could stop himself. But he knew he could never stop both of them. What should he do? Wouldn't it be better to save at least one life?

No way! If Jonah was going to die, then Billy wanted to die along with him. He let himself fall.

They flew over the bank of the creek, hit a rock midstream, and spun out of each other's grasp. Billy hit his head on the rock and felt his body twist in the rushing water. Jonah swept on by, heading toward a waterfall. Billy screamed as his friend shot by him and out of sight. Then, as he struggled for footing in the water, he saw Jonah's upraised hand downstream, reaching for a better hold. Jonah was still alive! He had been wedged behind a rock, just a few feet from the top of the falls.

Billy and Jonah crawled from the stream dripping wet and numb with cold. Darkness had descended; an inky, wilderness night hid the way back to safety. They still needed to get back to camp, but now—in addition to the cold and the darkness—they faced yet another obstacle: Jonah had injured both ankles in the river.

Now what? How much could two kids survive? As they staggered away from Milk Creek, Billy began seriously to wonder if they would ever make it back. Wouldn't it be wiser to wait—and hope for the best? Yes, they might lose their hands and feet to frostbite, but wouldn't that be better than losing their lives in another fall?

"Maybe…maybe we should stay down here and wait it out," Billy told Jonah.

"Whassa matter?" Jonah mumbled through cracked and swollen lips. "You a wimp or somethin'?"

"I—I don't think we're going to make it. I don't think we can go any further. We can't see. It's just too dark."

That was the moment Billy saw a glow shining from his friend's midsection.

"*What's that?*" Billy shouted. "What's that—in your pocket?"

"Oh!" said Jonah, staring dazedly at the gentle radiance beneath his wet pullover. "It's my flashlight!"

Jonah had forgotten about the small flashlight tucked in his front pocket. Somehow it too had survived the nine-hundred-foot plunge down the mountain and the subsequent tumble into the stream. And now, it had seemingly switched itself on.

This is from God, Billy thought to himself. *He's saying, "You're going to make it, and I'll show you the way."*

Jonah, too, took it as a sign. He knew the Lord had sent it to give them hope and help to carry on. They had to keep moving, keep climbing. And somehow they did. At half past two in the morning, the pair stumbled back into camp to await their rescuers.[1]

Some of God's miracles are huge and earthshaking, lighting up the sky. Others are quiet and tiny. Something as small as a weak moan at the bottom of an icy crevasse. Something as tiny as a glow of light at the last moment on a dark dead end....

Later, Jonah couldn't stop talking about God. Thanking Him. Praising Him. He knew he shouldn't be alive. Knew it wasn't some stroke of luck that had saved him. Knew it wasn't because he and Billy had been jocks, or tough-minded kids, or whatever else the news media had said. They could call it luck or pluck or whatever they wanted to. Jonah was very well aware that he was still alive because of the grace and mercy of God.

He had come to the darkest night of his young life and found God there, waiting for him at the dead end.

Jonah learned something about the grace and timing and strength and mercy of the Lord on the cold, unforgiving slopes of Mount Jefferson. He and Billy had come to a dead end, had no one to turn to but God, and found out that God was enough.

[1] For the chronology of these events I am indebted to the excellent article by Antje Spethmann in the August 31, 1995 issue of *The Oregonian*.

Ron Mehl is a pastor and author of Gold Medallion-winning God Works the Night Shift *and* Meeting God at a Dead End.

Great Balls of Fire

by Rodney Charles

The most popular evangelist of the Great Welsh Revival was Mary Jones, a thirty-five-year-old housewife from Egryn in North Wales. Whenever she preached, mysterious lights were seen in the sky, above or nearby her assembly. The lights, seen by thousands of witnesses, resembled bright stars or fireballs that "zigzagged" as they moved.

The following report was written by a journalist for the London Daily Mail who was sent to Egryn to cover the event.

"...At 8:14 P.M. I was on the hillside, walking from Dyffryn to Egryn. In the distance, about one mile away, I could see the three lighted windows of the tiny Egryn chapel, where the service was going on. It was the only light in the miles of countryside. Suddenly at 8:20 P.M. I saw what appeared to be a ball of fire above the roof of the chapel. It came from nowhere, and sprang into existence instantaneously. It had a steady, intense yellow brilliance, and did not move.

"Not sure whether or not I was deceiving myself, I called to a man a hundred yards down the road, and asked him if he could see anything. He came running to me excitedly and said, 'Yes, yes, above the chapel, the great light.' He was a countryman, and was trembling with emotion.

"We watched the light together. It seemed to me to be at twice the height of the chapel, say fifty feet, and it stood out with electric vividness against the encircling hills behind. Suddenly it disappeared, having lasted about a minute and a half.

"I leaned against the stone wall by the wayside and watched for further developments, the countryman leaving me and making his way alone. Again, the chapel windows were the only light in the countryside. The minutes crept by and it was 8:35 P.M. before I saw anything else. Then two lights flashed out, one on each side of the chapel. They seemed about a hundred feet apart and considerably higher than the first one. In the night it was difficult to judge distance, but I made a rough guess that they were a hundred feet above the roof of the chapel. They shone out brilliantly and steadily for a space of thirty seconds. Then they both began to flicker like a defective arc-lamp. They were flickering like that while one could count to ten...."

Rodney Charles is the Author of Every Day a Miracle Happens.

Miracles of
PRAYER

The miracles in fact are a retelling in small letters
of the very same story which is written across the whole world
in letters too large for some of us to see.

C.S. Lewis

Miracles of
PRAYER

L ike miracles, prayer is a mystery. How is God able to "hear" us? In what ways does prayer impact our relationship with him? Why is it that some prayers are seemingly "answered" while, with the limited realm of human perception, others appear to fall on deaf ears?

When we pray, we assume a number of things: that God exists, that he is listening, that he cares and responds. We hope that he will answer in the way we expect. But in reality, it rarely happens that way. We feel disappointed when God chooses a different course of action or, to our eyes, none at all. At such times, though we cannot see it, God *is* working in our lives. Often, answers to prayer come not in changed circumstances, but in changed hearts—something that happens when we open ourselves up in prayer.

At other times, God far exceeds our expectations, answering prayers in sensational, unbelievable—even theatrical—ways. In the face of such attention, it is easy to recognize that prayer brings results. For a moment, we can actually see God's hand moving as he works in our lives.

May the following stories of dramatic answers to prayer remind you of what the Lord can do, encourage you to develop the art of praying in your own life, and give you a greater desire to tap into the resources of God himself.

SELLING CATTLE

by Howard Hendricks

Shortly after Dallas Seminary was founded in 1924, it almost folded. It came to the point of bankruptcy. All the creditors were ready to foreclose at twelve noon on a particular day. That morning, the founders of the school met in the president's office to pray that God would provide. In that prayer meeting was Harry Ironside. When it was his turn to pray, he said in his refreshingly candid way, "Lord, we know that the cattle on a thousand hills are Thine. Please sell some of them and send us the money."

Just about that time, a tall Texan in boots and an open-collar shirt strolled into the business office. "Howdy!" he said to the secretary. "I just sold two carloads of cattle over in Fort Worth. I've been trying to make a business deal go through, but it just won't work. I feel God wants me to give this money to the seminary. I don't know if you need it or not, but here's the check," and he handed it over.

The secretary took the check and, knowing something of the critical nature of the hour, went to the door of the prayer meeting and timidly tapped. Dr. Lewis Sperry Chafer, the founder and president of the school, answered the door and took the check from her hand. When he looked at the amount, it was for the exact sum of the debt. Then he recognized the name on the check as that of the cattleman. Turning to Dr. Ironside, he said, "Harry, God sold the cattle."

Howard Hendricks is an author, professor and lecturer at Dallas Theological Seminary, and chairman for the Center for Christian Leadership

COVERED WITH A CLOUD

by Spencer January

It was 1945—I was twenty-four years old and in the U.S. Army's 35th Infantry. We were pushing hurriedly through the woods and towns in the Rhineland region of West Germany.

As my comrades and I cautiously made our way through a thickly wooded area, word came that the company ahead of us had been badly shot up by the enemy and that we were to replace them.

When my company arrived at the scene, I was appalled by the grimness of the situation. Only a handful of wounded, bleeding soldiers hiding behind a large stone house at the edge of the woods had survived. The route to Ossenburg had been completely barricaded.

"God," I prayed desperately, thinking of my wife and little son back home, "You've got to do something...please do something, God!"

Moments later, the order was given to advance. Just as the soldier ahead of me took a step, something caught my eye. I stopped and stared in amazement. A cloud—a long, fluffy, white cloud—had appeared instantly out of nowhere, obscuring the Germans' line of fire.

Taking advantage of this miraculous turn of events, I and my fellow soldiers bolted into the clearing and ran for our lives. Safe in the sheltering woods on the other side of the clearing, I hid behind a tree and exclaimed, "This has to be God! I'm going to see what happens now."

I watched closely as the last American soldier frantically raced toward us into the woods. I will never forget what happened next. The instant the soldier scrambled to safety, the cloud vanished! Poof! It was gone.

The Germans, thinking they still had the American soldiers pinned down behind the stone house on the other side of the field, radioed its position to their artillery. Minutes later, the house was blown to bits.

Two weeks later, a letter arrived from my mother back in Dallas, Texas. "Son, what in the world was the matter on the morning of March 9?" she asked. "You remember Mrs. Tankersly from our church? Well, she called me that morning and said that the Lord had awakened her at one o'clock in the night and said, 'Spencer is in serious trouble. Get up now and pray for him!' Mrs. Tankersly said she interceded for you until six o'clock the next morning. She told me that the last thing she prayed before getting off her knees, was, "Lord, whatever danger Spencer is in, just cover him with a cloud!'"

ANGRY GUARD DOGS

by Robert P. Dugan, Jr.

The third weekend in October 1992, I flew to Dallas, Texas to launch an annual lecture series at the Highland Park Presbyterian Church. That Sunday afternoon, I left my hotel to begin a fast five-mile walk, and within minutes was literally in fear for my life.

I had inadvertently entered private property, a one-hundred-year-old estate well known in north-central Dallas. As I became aware of my mistake, three fierce-looking black watchdogs came out of nowhere, headed full-bore for me. It may have been the wrong tactic, but I didn't freeze. Calling out, "Lord, save me!" I ran toward the house one hundred yards away, praying the owners would hear my shouts, throw open the doors, and call off the dogs. Two cars were parked there, but no one would be home.

One dog twice got his teeth into my calf, and I stumbled. "Please, Lord, don't let me fall." I had visions of being chewed upon and left to bleed to death. As the dogs chased me, they nipped but did not bite again, and then stopped at the steps—as if forbidden to come onto the porch. I stood trapped by three enraged, fearsome, high-decibel barking dogs—joined by other family-type dogs—but was temporarily safe. Either the dogs were trained to stay off the porch, or the small boxes on their collars prohibited their crossing a silent, electronic barrier.

After nearly a half-hour, my hollering for help was heard and police were called, but a good neighbor drove his car into the estate and rescued me before they could arrive. Two hours in the Presbyterian Hospital emergency room were sufficient to cleanse the puncture wounds under local anesthetic; to allow me thirty minutes to change; and to let me begin my Sunday evening address on time. Back home, with the help of antibiotics and daily cleansing, the wounds were healing nicely. Police animal control officers would later assure me that the Doberman-blend dogs did not have rabies.

The following Wednesday, in my office, I received a "Prayer Gram" card from Raleigh's Providence Baptist Church "Upper Room" prayer ministry, in North Carolina. "You have been prayed for today in our church prayer room," said the hand-written note from my friend George Uribe—as far as I knew at the time, the only person in that church who knew my name. On the card he noted: "But you are a shield around me, O Lord," Psalm 3:3. "May God shield you and protect you."

My wife Lynne is receptionist at our National Association of Evangelicals Office for Governmental Affairs. Handing me the card, she watched my face, then wondered aloud if I had noticed the date. My eyes shifted. October 18. Sunday!

I immediately phoned George. He was as enthused at this marvelous evidence of God's goodness as I was. God had prompted unknown brothers and sisters to pray for me on the exact day that my life was in jeopardy.

One thing more. Did George recall what time they had gathered to pray? Yes, he did. Somehow I knew what his answer would be. Four-thirty in North Carolina translated into 3:30 Central Daylight Time in Dallas—precisely the half-hour I left the Doubletree Hotel to go walking!

Robert P. Dugan, Jr. is Vice President at Large for the National Association of Evangelicals.

I Put "New Car" on My Prayer List

by Linda Rogers

Regrettably and sadly, my marriage of thirty-one years ended in divorce. I was stunned when we were unable to work things out and was subsequently served with divorce papers in August of 1991.

For thirty-one years I had been a stay-at-home wife and mother. I knew how to cross stitch, oil paint, crochet, and make a million great crock pot meals. But here I was out of my home with no financial support!

I was forty-six years old. I had no home, no furniture, no car, no kitchen items, no marketable skills, and now I had no husband! I thought to myself, *God has a real problem*, and I was terrified. Fortunately I was able to find work and a place to live.

In June of 1992, I put "new car" on my prayer list. Now I didn't really mean "new" car as in off the showroom floor—but a new car to me. The car I was driving was running out of time. Also, it wasn't a *neat* car, and I wanted a *neat* car!

I prayed consistently for my new car and continued to remind God how long I had been praying for it. I had no idea how He was going to do it, but He was my husband now, and I was His responsibility. However, I did know that He didn't want me to go into debt by purchasing a car.

Eventually I was awarded the proceeds from the sale of my former home. When I received this news, I knew I would soon be getting a new car. I told my friends that God had already picked it out, and it was just a matter of waiting to see what kind of car it would be.

About that time, a friend at work purchased a new car and was offering his "old" car for sale—a 1992 Buick Park Avenue Ultra with 46,000 miles. Now that's a new car to me!

Since we work in the same ministry, I stopped by his office and asked about the Buick. I told him I was planning to buy a car with all the bells and whistles, and although I didn't have the money yet, I was starting to look.

Knowing there is safety in several counselors (Proverbs 11:14), I talked with two friends (separately) about how to handle the negotiations. Without knowing about each other, they made identical recommendations. I made a list and then asked God to arrange for the friend with the Buick to come into my office when the time was right for me to speak to him.

Two days later there was a knock at my office door and there he stood. He wanted to speak with me about a work-related matter, but I knew God had arranged this meeting. When he finished with his reason for the visit, I asked him if we could talk about his Buick and he agreed.

I told him about my situation and made him an offer. He promptly refused it as being too low. I asked him not to counter the offer yet but to pray about it with his wife.

The next morning, he asked me what I had prayed the night before. I told him I had asked God to make it crystal clear what he and his wife should do regarding the Buick and me. He said that God had awakened them at 1:00 A.M. and by 2:20 A.M. they knew exactly what they were supposed to do.

He proceeded to give me the keys and signed the title over to me. God had made it clear to them, he said, that the Buick was my car. I reminded him that I did not have the money yet.

"No problem," he replied. "Give me a check when you receive the money. And by the way, we will not accept your offer." He then proceeded to sell the car to me for less than my offer (which was extremely low to begin with).

"Linda, God wants you to have this car," he said. "This is His gift to you. My wife and I really have nothing to do with this gift; we just happen to have the keys. Go pick it up today. The car is yours!"

The next evening, at my Bible study group, I told them the story, showing them the notation in my prayer journal which listed *new car, June 1992*. One of the men said, "Come outside and let's look at something." He opened the door on the driver's side where the date of manufacture is listed. It read *June 1992*.

When I told my friend about the date the car was manufactured he said, "Well thanks, Linda, for letting me drive *your* car for three years!"

"No problem," I replied.

Linda Rogers is a Development Officer with Walk Thru the Bible Ministries.

Twenty-Seven Soldiers

by Billy Graham

A missionary and his family were forced to camp outside on a hill. They had money with them and were fearful of an attack by roving thieves. After praying, they went to sleep. Months later an injured man was brought to the mission hospital. He asked the missionary if he had soldiers guarding him on that night. "We intended to rob you," he said, "but we were afraid of the twenty-seven soldiers."

When the missionary returned to his homeland, he related this story, and a member of the church said, "We had a prayer meeting that night, and I took the roll. There were just twenty-seven of us present." Prayers have no boundaries. They can leap miles and continents and be translated instantly into any language.

Billy Graham is a world renowned evangelist and best-selling author.

Danger in the Canyon

by Andrea Gross

As Shirley Halliday unlocked the door to her home in Hartland, Michigan, she realized she was truly alone for the first time in her adult life. Three months earlier, in May 1976, her husband had died. Now her thirteen-year-old daughter, Janie, the youngest of her six children and the only one still living at home, was away on vacation with one of her older brothers.

Shirley, a nurse, had just finished working the night shift at the hospital. As she prepared for her morning devotion, a strange feeling came over her. She knew—absolutely *knew*—that Janie was in danger. An icy cold swept over her, and wrenching sobs shook her body.

Meanwhile, more than fifteen hundred miles away, Janie had wandered away from her brother and sister-in-law, fascinated by her first view of the Painted Desert. Standing at the top of a ravine so deep she couldn't see the bottom, she thought the Arizona landscape looked like something from another world. She stepped over the low guardrail to get a better view—and lost her footing.

Tumbling down the sloping canyon walls, Janie frantically

tried to grab onto something, anything to slow her descent, but the rock was weathered and slippery, and the sand that covered it offered almost no traction. Janie began sliding faster and faster, swept toward certain death.

Back in Michigan, Shirley, in desperation, called on the angels to save her daughter. Aloud, she read Psalm 91:11–12: "For He shall give His angels charge over you, to keep you in all your ways. They shall bear you up in their hands, lest you dash your foot against a stone" (NKJV). As the family later reconstructed the scene, it was at the exact moment when Shirley finished her prayers that Janie miraculously slid to a stop, fifty yards from where she had fallen.

Her face white and her hands scraped from grabbing at the rocky cliff, Janie looked around. What had halted her? There were no protrusions in the canyon wall or clumps of vegetation to break her fall. It was as if an invisible hand had reached across her path and caught her.

With no help in sight, the dazed girl slowly inched her way back up by sitting down and pushing herself backward, ignoring the dirt and gravel embedded in her legs and the smashed camera in her back pocket. As Janie reached the top—where her frantic relatives would soon find her—Shirley felt overwhelmed by a great sense of peace. She knew her daughter was safe now.

Both Janie, now twenty-nine and an interior designer, and Shirley, who has since remarried, are still awed by what they believe is a miracle. "From that moment I knew that the Lord watches over the widow and is father to the fatherless," says Shirley. "I had no fear about raising my youngest child alone because I was confident that I had the help of God and his angels."

Andrea Gross is a contributing editor to Ladies Home Journal.

THE SILENT ALARM

by Doris Sanford

G oing to China with her husband and baby son was both exhilarating and frightening. This was not a tour. It was a lifetime commitment to the unknown. She and Mac had been in Bible school, raised their support, and said their official good-byes at church. They would leave next week by ship for language school on the coast of China before going to their final destination in the northern interior of China.

For Lillian the hardest part of leaving was saying good-bye to her closest friends. Beulah was one of the close ones. They wept and reminded each other that if they didn't meet again on this earth, that for sure they would be together in heaven and have eternity to talk. As a final gesture of her deep love for Lillian, Beulah promised to allow God to awaken her any hour of the day or night during the next four-year term when Mac and Lillian or the baby were in need of prayer. She showed Lillian the prayer journal she had prepared. She promised to write the date, time of day, and any special thoughts she had each time she felt a need to pray for them. Lillian also agreed to keep a written record of specific times when someone in the family was in need of prayer.

There were no phone calls, no e-mail, not even regular mail. The news that came was mostly in the newspaper or on the radio, and that news was not good. There was the Communist invasion of northern China; massacre of American missionaries; schools for missionary children turned into POW camps. The news was clearly not good.

Although Beulah did not hear directly from Lillian more than a few times a year, she knew that they must be in danger because she was losing a lot of sleep being awakened at night with an urgent desire to pray.

In China, Mac and Lillian and son were living on the run, hiding out in caves in the mountains, traveling at night over steep mountain passes on donkeys, going without medical care for serious illness. They survived by being hidden by Chinese Christians. Their close friends, another missionary couple, had already been martyred. On various scraps of paper Lillian jotted down dates, times, and the terrifying danger.

Four years later, at a kitchen table, the journals were laid side by side. Through tears and laughter the two women compared their notes. Dates, times, and events in northern China matched exactly with silent alarms that had brought a friend to her knees in a small town in Oregon.

Doris Sanford is the author of more than a dozen books and a teacher of psychiatric nursing

Miracles of

HEALING

Jesus never met a disease he could not cure,

a birth defect he could not reverse,

a demon he could not exorcise.

But he did meet skeptics he could not convince

and sinners he could not convert.

Philip Yancey

Miracles of
HEALING

We've all heard stories of miraculous, unexplained healings: the young mother whose brain tumor "disappeared" overnight; the crippled child who woke up one morning with the ability to walk; the husband whose broken back appeared to have "healed itself."

While friends and family of the "healed" rejoice, the rest of us smile, scratch our heads, and try to make sense of it all. Certainly, we're happy when healing takes place. But we can't help but wonder: "How did it happen? Did the doctors make a mistake in the original diagnosis? Isn't there some *logical* explanation for what has occurred?" In our eagerness to find rational answers, we often lose sight of miracles unfolding before our very eyes.

While stories of physical healing abound, their provability is more difficult. That God heals is indisputable; that every "miraculous" healing is a miracle is doubtful. Mistakes do occur, and false claims are made. Yet our inability to investigate and verify each claim should not keep us from recognizing the truth that *God can and does heal.*

Scriptural accounts tell us that Jesus gave special attention to the sick. He seemed touched by their need; at times, his compassion alone prompted him to heal. But he often had a greater purpose. After giving sight to the blind man, Jesus made sure the people understood that the man's blindness had not been caused by sin; it had been allowed as an opportunity for God to be glorified. In healing the paralytic, Jesus also forgave the man's sins, setting the stage for a discussion in which he compared the ease with which sins can be forgiven to the power to grant physical healing.

Perhaps the best question to ask in such situations is not, "Is what happened really a miracle?" but, "What does God want to teach me through this experience?" For when our hearts are changed, more than just the body is healed.

And those are among the greatest miracles of all.

ANGEL ON HER SHOULDER

by Andrea Gross

Please, somebody help me! My baby's not breathing!"
screamed Carole Moore as she ran into the hallway of her
apartment building. Why wasn't anyone answering?

Just a few minutes earlier, the magazine editor had been sitting peacefully in her living room in New York trying to amuse
her daughters: Julie, almost three, and Allison, eighteen
months. Allison was uncharacteristically fussy and cried in
spite of her mother's efforts to comfort her. The toddler's wails
grew louder and louder—and then suddenly stopped.

Allison slumped over, her lips turning blue from lack of
oxygen. Carole frantically started pounding her on the back.
"Breathe, Allison! Breathe!" She grabbed the limp child and
headed for the hallway. "Can't somebody help me?"

Carole, who describes herself as "not particularly religious,"
wasn't looking for divine intervention—just someone who
knew first aid. But although there were usually plenty of people
in the neighboring apartments, on this particular day in the
spring of 1990, no one answered her cries.

Suddenly Carole felt a deep calm settle over her. "Relax,
Carole," she said to herself. "You took the class in child safety

last year. You know what to do." As Julie watched, wide-eyed, from the doorway, Carole lay Allison on the hall floor, leaned over her, and began mouth-to-mouth resuscitation. The child soon responded. "My terror just disappeared," Carole says. "Something took over, and it was almost like I had stepped outside of myself. I could see myself doing what I had to do."

That night, after the doctor had diagnosed Allison's illness as croup and the baby was sleeping peacefully, Julie crawled into her mother's lap. "Mommy," she asked quietly, "who was that man who had his hand on your shoulder?"

"What man, honey?" Carole asked.

"The *man*, Mommy. The man who had his hand on your shoulder while you were helping Allison breathe."

Although Julie couldn't describe the stranger—except to say she was sure it was a man, not a woman—he'd obviously made a deep impression on her. After six weeks of questioning her mother daily, the little girl burst into tears of frustration. "Mommy, why can't you tell me about the man?" she asked, sobbing.

Carole hugged her daughter close. "I didn't see the man, honey," she said. "That's why I can't explain him to you."

Andrea Gross is a contributing editor for Ladies Home Journal.

BEAUTIFUL EYES

by Adrian Rogers

believe God does heal today—sovereignly, supernaturally, radically, and dramatically. In fact, I want to tell you about a precious friend I have known for twenty years. Her name is Marolyn Ford, and her story is an incredible testimony to the healing power of God.

As a young lady, Marolyn began to lose her eyesight. It progressively got worse and worse. The doctor told her she had an irreversible problem called macular deterioration. He predicted that it would progress until she would be legally blind. This indeed happened. She lost her sight and had to go to a school for the blind and learn to tap with a cane and read Braille.

But the story does not end there. She went away to Bible college to study. The professors allowed her to take classes with a tape recorder. There, as a sightless young girl, she met a young ministerial student named Acie Ford. They fell in love, and this young preacher married a bride who was beautiful but could not see her bridegroom.

God gave them a little baby. She could not see the face of her baby either. God gave them a wonderful church, and she knew her church members by voice but could not see their faces.

Marolyn had prayed many times that she might be healed by miracle or medicine, but nothing seemed to help. One evening after a time of ministry, she and her husband were driving home late at night. They discussed Marolyn's blindness. Acie talked to her about the impediment it was to the ministry and how wonderful it would be if God would heal her. Let Marolyn tell you what happened in her own words, taken from her book, *These Blind Eyes Now See*:

> That evening both of us were exhausted. Acie picked up a religious periodical, and I climbed into bed. After reading for a minute, Acie put the magazine down, got on his knees for our nightly devotion, and began praying.
>
> We both began to cry as he prayed with great feeling and boldness: "Oh, God! You can restore Marolyn's eyesight tonight, Lord. I know You can do it! And, God, if it be Your will, I pray You will do it tonight." Perhaps neither of us was quite prepared for what happened. After twelve blurred and dark years, there was sharpness and light.
>
> "Acie, I can see!" I exclaimed.
>
> "You're kidding," he answered.
>
> I repeated, "I can see! I can see the pupils in your eyes!"
>
> Acie thought that perhaps just a little vision had come back.
>
> I said, "Acie, it's 12:30 at night. You need a shave! I can see!"
>
> Acie still couldn't believe the miracle that had really occurred. He grabbed a newspaper, pointed to the large print at the top of the page, and asked, "Can you see this?" "I can do better than that!" I exclaimed. "I can read the smaller print!"
>
> Acie got excited. "Marolyn, can you see the dresser? Can you see the bed?"

We shouted and praise the Lord for what He had done! Such a miracle was overwhelming. Things had been rough for Acie lately as he tried to keep up with both his church work and his sales job. He had nearly reached his limit that evening when the miracle happened. We knew that God was able, but we couldn't comprehend that something so wonderful and miraculous had happened to us.

Jumping off the bed, Acie asked the question again, "Marolyn, can you see?"

"Yes!"

"Praise God! Praise God! Praise God! Glory, glory, glory to God! It can't be!" Acie exclaimed.

We were beside ourselves with happiness. "This is heaven!" Acie shouted. "It has to be! Oh, God, why did I doubt You?"

Then he turned to me. "Why did I doubt God? I didn't believe He could do something like this! He did it!"

Psalm 116:12—"What shall I render unto the LORD for all his benefits toward me?" (KJV)—came to Acie's mind. We were jumping up and down and crying at the same time. I was getting my first look at my husband. For the first time, I could see his face, his eyes, his nose, his mouth. I could see!

I ran to look in the mirror. I could hardly believe how my facial features had changed. I had become blind at nineteen; now I was thirty-one. I kept taking a second look....

We reached for the phone to call our parents. When the phone rang at my parents' home in Michigan, Mother was awake—she had not been able to sleep that night. For years she had been burdened with the thought of my blindness and her own helplessness in not being able to do anything about it. How happy our news made her! She rejoiced with us over *the telephone lines. I asked her to share the news with the others in my family who lived in Holland, Michigan and with my twin sister in New York.*

Acie dialed his parents, and his mother sleepily answered. Acie shouted, "Mother, Marolyn can see!"

Mom Ford had been awakened in the middle of the night by a son too excited to speak calmly. She asked, "Is everything all right?" But Acie could only repeat over and over: "Marolyn can see! Marolyn can see! She can see!"

We tried to explain to Mom and Dad Ford, but we had so little time. There were many other phone calls to make. We wanted to run down the street at 1 A.M. and shout that I was blind, but now I see!

The director for the school for the blind said she should go to the doctor and let him confirm this miracle.

The doctor who had examined her before in her blindness put the eye charts in front of her. She read them with ease. He said to her, "I cannot doubt or deny that you can see. Now let me look into your eyes."

When he did, he gave a gasp. He said, "I don't understand it. There is really no change. A portion of your eyes are like mirror that had the quicksilver scraped off." He said it was a bigger miracle than he would have believed. "It is impossible for you to see and yet you see."

In the years since then, Marolyn has crossed America giving her testimony. It has blessed and strengthened thousands. She does not believe it is always God's will to heal, but she cannot deny what God has done for her.

I am blessed continually when I am around this humble and dedicated couple who have seen God do a miracle. To look into Marolyn's beautiful blue eyes gives one the feeling that he is seeing with his own eyes an undeniable, supernatural work of God.

Adrian Rogers Pastor of a 28,000-member church in Memphis, Tennessee; three-time president of Southern Baptist Convention; founder of "Love Worth Finding," a TV and radio ministry; and author of many books including Believe in Miracles but Trust in Jesus.

GETTING STRAIGHTENED OUT

by Tony Campolo

everal years ago, I was invited to be a guest lecturer at a small college in the Midwest. It was one of those schools that had been founded by religious people but had lost its religious mooring. While the school had become secularized, there were a few remaining signs of its previous religious affiliation. One of them was an annual religious emphasis week. Most religious colleges have such weeks in which an effort is made to religiously "psych up" the student body. Usually these efforts produce little change. This particular student body thought that I could do the job for them and brought me in to resurrect their dead. My assignment was to interest an apathetic student body that was forced to attend my lectures about how Christianity was supposedly exciting and intellectually tenable.

The college had scheduled the lectures for evenings. At the end of my presentation on the second night a woman came down the aisle of the auditorium carrying her child in her arms. The child was crippled and in braces, and the woman was obviously not a member of the student body. Furthermore, she had a strange look in her eyes.

"What do you want?" I asked.

She answered, "God told me to come."

I didn't know how to handle that. It seemed to me that if God had told her to come, the least He could have done was to tell me that she was coming.

I asked, "Well, is there something you think I can do for you?"

She said, "You're supposed to heal my child."

I responded, "Dear lady, I don't have the gift of healing. There are a variety of gifts according to the Bible. Some people are given the gift of tongues, some the gift of prophesy, some the gift of healing and some the gift of teaching. Teaching is my gift."

I had the strong inclination to simply point to my bald head and say, "If I could heal, would I look like this?" I told her that healing just was not my thing, but she wouldn't back off. "God told me to come," she said even more emphatically.

The students quickly picked up what was happening, and I could hear whispers and titters of laughter spread over the audience. There was no question that they were delighted to see my discomfort. The chaplain of the college recognized that I was in an embarrassing situation. He was the typical college chaplain. I'm sure you know the type. They wear turtleneck sweaters, and chains with big crosses around their necks. They smoke pipes and then try to look very relevant. He came over to us and he asked, "What's the problem, Doctor?"

I said, "This lady wants me to heal her kid."

He asked, "Do you want some help?"

"Please!" I shot back.

The chaplain spoke to the audience and said, "Those who do not believe that this child is going to be healed this evening, please leave the auditorium. If you are not absolutely convinced that this child will have his legs straightened through prayer, I want you to get out of here. Not even Jesus could perform miracles or mighty works when He was surrounded by people who were filled with unbelief."

Hey, I thought to myself, *that's not bad for a theologically liberal college chaplain. That's really a smart move.*

It was a smart move, because once he said that, almost everyone in the auditorium got up and left. With one statement he had cleared the place. All that were left were five Pentecostal kids, and they were already into their thing, lifting hands into the air and praying in tongues. I figured the guy had gotten me off the hook, that I was safe and clear.

I asked, "What do we do now?"

He answered, "We're taking the kid out back into the kitchen."

"What are you going to do in the kitchen?" was my response.

He said, "We're going to anoint the child's head with oil."

"Oil? What kind of oil?"

"Del Monte!" he answered with a smile on his face.

Somehow that answer lacked the kind of spirituality that I was expecting. I thought he might have something like holy water from Israel or some special ointment that had been blessed by the pope.

I asked, "Are you kidding?"

He said, "Look, Campolo; it says in the Book of James that if somebody needs healing, the elders of the church are to anoint the person's head with oil, lay hands on him, and pray for healing. So, unless you have a better idea, you had better do what the Book tells you."

Now that is not bad advice, no matter what the source. So we went into the back room and did what we were supposed to do. We followed the instructions in the Book of James like it was a cookbook. First we applied the oil, then we laid on our hands, and then we prayed. I had invited the five Pentecostal kids to join us, so they had their hands on the kid's head too. I figured that if anybody had anything going for him, I wanted him in on this.

I started to pray. It was one of those phony prayers that are all too common when we pray in the presence of others. I think you know what I mean. So often when others are present, we have a tendency to utter pat religious phrases that are high-sounding and that communicate an image of spirituality rather than concentrating on God. I can still hear myself praying: "O God, the great Creator of the Universe; O thou who in the days of old has healed the blind, made the lame to walk and raised up the dead, we beseech Thee in this hour to be present among us—" And I stopped dead. In the midst of my prayer my Pentecostal friends stopped their praying in tongues. We all felt it. We all felt a strange and awesome presence break loose in our midst. The Holy Spirit had descended into our midst. His Presence was overpowering and disturbing and shattered my pretended religiosity. The experience must have been something similar to what Isaiah described in the sixth chapter of his book. There he said,

In the year that King Uzziah died I saw the Lord sitting upon a throne, high and lifted up; and his train filled the temple. Above him stood the seraphim; each had six wings: with two he covered his face, and with two he covered his feet, and with two he flew. And one called to another and said: "Holy, holy, holy is the LORD of hosts; the whole earth is full of his glory." And the foundations of the thresholds shook at the voice of him who called, and the house was filled with smoke. And I said: "Woe is me! For I am lost; for I am a man of unclean lips, and I dwell in the midst of a people of unclean lips; for my eyes have seen the King, the LORD of hosts!" (Isaiah 6:1–5, RSV)

It is an awesome thing to stand in the presence of the Almighty. I didn't know how to react. Instinctively, I removed my hand and I felt terribly ashamed. My Pentecostal friends withdrew their hands too. I must admit that I fully expected that the child would be healed. The power of the Spirit was so overwhelming that a miraculous healing would not have surprised me. But the child was not healed. After some awkward excuses and explanations we all got out of the room and I quickly left the building. The rest of the lectures in the series unfolded in a very uneventful way. I was glad when the week was over and I could get back to my home, away from that strange and mysterious situation.

Three years after that I was a guest speaker in a church in St. Louis. When the worship service was over a lady came up to me and asked, "Do you remember me?"

"Yes!" I answered. "It was three years ago that I met you. You brought your little boy for healing. We prayed for him. How is your little boy?"

She said, "I came here today because I wanted you to see him. Here he is."

There beside her, with no braces on his legs, her little boy was standing as straight and as whole as any boy could be. His legs weren't twisted anymore.

"How did this happen?" I asked.

She answered, "We prayed! Don't you remember? We prayed! The next morning he woke up crying. I noticed that his braces were a little tight. I loosened them and his legs straightened just a little. It happened again the next morning, and then it happened again and again and again. It kept happening until his legs were made straight."

I didn't know how to handle any of that. The situation was beyond me.

A few days later I was back in my hometown, Philadelphia, having lunch with two academic colleagues. One was a professor of religion from the University of Pennsylvania. I explained to my friends what had happened, and one of them said, "Well, Tony, I have to be honest with you. My theology does not allow for that sort of thing to happen." Isn't that wild? I mean, you've got to smile at that response. *His* theology did not allow for that to happen!

I said, "Charlie, I don't want to upset you, but maybe—just maybe—God is able to do abundantly more than your theology could ever hope or think."

Tony Campolo is an author and Professor of Sociology at Eastern College in Saint Davids, Pennsylvania.

OUR DAUGHTER'S CANCER

by Henry T. Blackaby

Our daughter Carrie's bout with cancer was a difficult circumstance for our whole family. The doctors prepared us for six or eight months of chemotherapy plus radiation. We knew God loved us. We prayed, "What are you purposing to do in this experience that we need to adjust ourselves to?"

As we prayed, a Scripture promise came that we believed was from God. Not only did we receive the promise, but we received letters and calls from many people who quoted this same Scripture. The verse reads, "This sickness is not unto death, but for the glory of God, that the Son of God may be glorified through it" (John 11:4, NKJV).

Our sense that God was speaking to us grew stronger as the Bible, prayer, and the testimony of other believers began to line up and say the same thing. We then adjusted our lives to the truth and began to watch for ways God would use the situation for His glory.

During this time, people from many places in Canada, Europe, and the United States began praying for Carrie. Individuals, college student groups, and churches called to tell us of their prayers. Many said something like this: "Our prayer life (prayer ministry) has become so dry and cold. We haven't seen any special answers to prayer in a long time. But when we heard about Carrie, we put her on our prayer list."

After *three* months of treatments, the doctors ran more tests. They said, "We don't understand this, but all the tests are negative. We cannot find any trace of the cancer." I immediately began to contact those who had committed to pray for Carrie, and shared with them this demonstration of prayer being answered. In instance after instance, people said that seeing God answer prayer totally renewed their prayer life. Church prayer ministries were revitalized. Student prayer groups found new life.

Then I began to see what God had in mind for this circumstance. Through this experience God was glorified in the eyes of His people. Many, many people sensed a fresh call to prayer.

We faced a trying situation. We could have looked back at God from the middle of that and gotten a very distorted understanding of God. Instead we went to Him.

Henry T. Blackaby is Director of Prayer and Spiritual Awakening, Southern Baptist Convention Home Mission Board, and co-author of Experiencing God.

BURIED ALIVE!

by Beth Mullally

Eugene Zerbe chipped ice off his windshield while his '86 Chevy Cavalier was warming up in the parking lot of the P.J. Valves Company in Myerstown, Pennsylvania. It was the fifteenth major storm of the season, and the heavy snow was mixing with sleet.

When Zerbe, a machinist, had punched out a few minutes earlier, his timecard said 4:31 P.M., Wednesday, March 2, 1994. His wife, Sandra, would be putting supper on the table at 5:30, as she did every evening.

In the nearly thirty years he'd been commuting over Blue Mountain to his home in Pine Grove, Pennsylvania, Zerbe, 57, had never seen a winter like this. Rather than take his usual short-cut home over a rural country road, he decided to make the twenty-mile trip over the 1450-foot mountain on the well traveled Route 501.

Driven by 50 mph winds, the sleet was getting worse as he turned onto 501 north. As Zerbe crept along the slippery road toward the mountain, ice thickened on his windshield. He was not alarmed—driving home in ice and snow had become routine this winter—but it struck him as odd that no cars were coming from the opposite direction.

It took a half-hour to travel the five miles to the flat stretch of road leading to the base of the mountain. Here the highway opened up, and wide-open fields flanked either side. He suddenly understood why he had seen no cars in the southbound lane—already, ice-encrusted drifts buried the road under two feet of snow. He began to notice trapped cars on both sides of the road.

Suddenly, Zerbe's blue Chevy came to a dead stop, caught fender-deep in a drift. His tires spun futilely. He tried to rock the car back and forth between forward and reverse. It wouldn't budge.

Sandra Zerbe checked the turkey roasting in the oven, then looked out the window at the snow, thinking of Eugene. From the moment she first saw him, she knew he was the man she would marry. When she moved to Pine Grove as a teenager, she noticed that he and his friends had a favorite street corner. She'd stroll by, hoping the handsome, dark-haired fellow would notice her. Eventually he did.

Now, married thirty-five years, she and Eugene had raised four children—Kim, Tim, Jim, and Eugene II ("Chuck")—who were all grown with families of their own. As Sandra waited, Kim, who lived nearby, appeared at the door.

"I'm sure he's okay," Sandra told her. The two women took turns telling each other there was nothing to worry about.

Dressed only in coveralls, sneakers and his medium-weight work jacket, Zerbe got out of his car to begin chipping away at the ice. He quickly realized he had made a mistake. Stunned by the wind's force, he had to hold on to the door with his ungloved hands to remain upright. The freezing pellets stung his skin and soaked his clothing, plastering his coveralls to his legs and weighing down his jacket.

Retreating inside, he watched the storm with growing anxiety. The snow was building so rapidly that in only fifteen minutes a drift piled up above the top of the window.

A half-hour later, he heard snowmobile engines. Soon a face covered by a ski mask peered through his window. "Any women or children in there with you?" the snowmobiler asked. He and five others had been called out to evacuate stranded motorists, women and children first.

"I'm alone," Zerbe replied. "I'm okay—just wet and cold."

"There's a front-loader up ahead pulling cars out of the drift," the snowmobiler said. "He'll be along for you. Just sit tight."

Over three miles away, Dave Bernhard, the road-crew foreman, watched as the operator of a front-loader tried to work the machine into the drift. In his fifteen years with the state Department of Transportation, he had never seen snow pile up so quickly. In only a few minutes it had drifted to a depth of six feet, covering all but the radio antennas of cars stranded on the highway. Plows were useless.

Riding on top of the drifts, the snowmobilers eventually evacuated seventy people from their cars. They believed they had gotten everyone, and had—except Zerbe. When they returned to his stretch of the road, they saw nothing but snow and left the scene. No one imagined that a man was entombed beneath the ice-encrusted snow.

Kim called the state police every half-hour. Each time the dispatcher told her, "No word yet. If anyone spots his car, we'll let you know."

Finally, at midnight, the dispatcher had some news. A four-mile section of Route 501 had been closed due to drifting.

Motorists were being evacuated, and the Mount Aetna fire-house was being set up as an emergency shelter.

Kim and her mother breathed small sighs of relief. Yet they thought it was strange that Eugene hadn't called to say he was all right. Sandra sent her daughter home at 2 A.M. with a promise to call the minute she had word. She read the Bible for a few minutes, then lay down to sleep.

Zerbe pulled his mini-flashlight out of his pocket to check the time—2:15 A.M. It had been a while since he'd heard the snowmobiles.

He was tempted to get out of the car again, but his wet clothes were a reminder that he'd accomplished nothing the first time. And by now a mountain of snow was leaning in on his car door.

His body began to tremble with cold, his hands shaking so badly he had trouble putting the key in the ignition. He couldn't leave the car running for long, as the fuel gauge showed nearly empty, but he wanted the heat on for a few minutes so he would stop shivering.

Zerbe shut down the engine and leaned back in his seat. *They'll come back for me*, he told himself, drifting off to sleep.

By 7:30 A.M., despite the raging storm, Sandra's house was filled with concerned relatives.

"We're going to find him," Tim said. Knowing no ordinary vehicle would make the trip, he had an idea: since both he and Chuck were members of the National Guard, they could borrow one of its trucks.

Bundled against the weather, Tim and Chuck walked to the local armory and clambered into an Army truck. By 9:30 they had picked up Kim and Jim and were heading south on Route 501 toward Blue Mountain. They soon found themselves in an eerie, wintery wasteland, where visibility was only a few feet.

Inching their way along at five mph, the Zerbes took two hours to travel ten miles up the mountain and down the other side. As they continued another mile south, they approached the northern edge of the drift. It looked like the wall of a glacier.

A state policeman flagged the truck down, "This is as far as you're going," he told them. "There's no way to get through for the next four miles." A front-end loader at the edge of the drift, scooping snow a bucketful at a time, was making scant progress.

"How soon before we'll be able to get through here?" Tim asked.

"Maybe Saturday," the trooper replied.

Two days! What if Dad was somewhere in that drift? "We'll go around," Kim said. Tim turned the truck back on 501 heading north. Before reaching the mountain, he turned onto another route leading to Myerstown so he could pick up 501 on the other side of the drift and retrace the route he believed his father had taken. But the truck reached another wall of snow.

Kim was overcome with despair. "How are we ever going to get to him?" she whispered.

"We'll walk," said Chuck. With less snow blowing and clearer visibility, he and Jim got out of the truck and groped their way to the top of the drift. Snow was piled halfway up telephone poles, and there was no other sign that this had ever been a road. In the distance they saw a snowmobile heading their way.

Dale Swope had been working much of the night, shuttling people from their cars to the Mount Aetna firehouse. "There's no one out there," Swope told the Zerbes when he approached them. "Your father had to be on some other road."

Devastated, the Zerbes headed home. For the first time, Kim began to wonder if her father was still alive.

Not 2000 feet away from where Chuck and Jim had stood, Zerbe sat in his buried car. *Got to warm up,* he thought, surprised at how slow his fingers responded when he moved them toward the ignition key. The trembling had stopped during the night, but now a deep numbness had overtaken him. Finally he turned his wrist and the engine came to life. Zerbe sat back while the car warmed up.

He felt groggy and disoriented as if he'd been drugged. Only gradually did he notice the smell. *Exhaust fumes! The pipe must be iced over. I could die of carbon-monoxide poisoning!*

He shut off the engine, then groped clumsily for the window crank. Only as he rolled down the window did Zerbe realize to his horror that his entire car was encased in ice.

Panicking, Zerbe clawed and pounded at the sharp, jagged snow. *I have to get air*, he thought frantically. Groping beneath the seats, he discovered an ice scraper. Panting with exertion and fear, he began chipping his way upward inch by inch, ice flying in his face. Finally he broke through to the surface, the tiniest of holes in his icy tomb.

He leaned back, laughing, and breathed deeply of the fresh air. But his exhilaration was short-lived. He could sense the air growing colder as the biting wind snaked downward through the opening. His clothes, still wet from the night before, began to freeze on his body. *I could die of hypothermia*, he thought.

With the cold overtaking his body, Zerbe sank into reverie. He knew there was nothing more he could do. *Please help me, God*, he prayed.

As Zerbe's body temperature began to decrease, blood flow to his extremities slowed, leaving them numb, while the flow remained strong throughout his midsection to protect his vital organs from the assault of the cold. His heart rate and respiration slowed and his blood pressure plummeted. Slowly, he faded into unconsciousness. And, gradually, Zerbe's body temperature dropped toward death.

Sandra sent her relatives home before midnight. By now Eugene had been missing for thirty-two hours. She spent the night sleepless, curled on the couch, begging God to bring her husband home to her.

Shortly after 8 A.M. on Friday, road crews began marking the presence of buried cars with orange traffic cones. As Dave Bernhard trudged through what appeared to be an empty expanse of snow, he spotted a small hole. He knelt down to peer in, and to his surprise he discovered another car.

Scooping away the snow, he cleared a large enough hole so he could press his face against the car window. Inside, an ashen-faced man was leaning back in the driver's seat. His eyes were rolled back in his head. At first Bernhard suspected the man was dead, but then he saw his head move slightly. "Hey!" Bernhard shouted. "Can you hear me? Hang on!" There was no answer.

Bernhard scrambled over to the loader working nearby. "I found someone buried in a car!" he shouted. Instructing the loader operator to start digging, Bernhard went to his truck and radioed for help. Then he grabbed two shovels and ran back.

The loader lumbered over, and the driver began digging, slowly exposing the blue car. Other rescuers arrived by snow-mobile, and several men jumped down into the cleared hole to help dig the last foot out by hand. "We're going to help you!" they shouted to the unconscious man inside.

After twenty-five minutes rescuers cleared the driver's door, but it wouldn't open. Peering in the window, Bernhard saw that it was locked. And with Zerbe slumped behind the wheel, the rescuers didn't dare break the window.

Since they had removed enough snow from the left rear window, they broke through it. The loader operator reached in and opened the front door lock. It was 9 A.M. Zerbe had been trapped inside the car for forty hours.

Pulling Zerbe from the car, the rescuers hoisted him over their heads to the others at the top, who laid him in the snowmobile driven by Dale Swope. "Let's go!" shouted Swope, noticing that Zerbe's legs were stiffened in position, and his socks were frozen to his legs.

Zerbe was delivered to the firehouse in fifteen minutes. His frozen clothing was removed, his body surrounded with warm packs, and warm fluids were pumped through a needle inserted in his arm. His temperature had dropped to 85 degrees, less than two degrees from probable death.

Zerbe responded swiftly. His heart rate returned to normal and his blood pressure rose. His breathing became deeper and more regular. Soon his face took on color and life.

Finally Zerbe opened his eyes and looked at the crowd of worried faces around him. "You're going to be okay, Mr. Zerbe," a paramedic reassured him. "We're taking you to the hospital." But Zerbe didn't say anything—he couldn't remember how to form words. Soon a helicopter flew him to Hershey Medical Center, thirty miles away.

By the time his family joined him in the emergency room an hour later, Zerbe was showing small signs of recovery. Sandra and their four children stood tense and silent while Dr. John Field tested his mental state.

"Can you tell me your name?" the doctor asked.

After a long pause, Zerbe finally spoke. "I'm Eugene Zerbe."

To the amazement of the hospital staff, Zerbe would be declared fully recovered and sent home three days later. Dr. Field agreed that medical science alone could not explain Zerbe's incredible survival. "Faith was at work here," Sandra Zerbe declared.

Miracle in My Family

by Dale Hanson Bourke

I am not sure that I ever really believed in miracles—until one happened in my own family.

It's not that I didn't believe in God or see him at work in my life. It's just that I had never before personally witnessed a moment when God intervened and upset the course of nature. In my heart I knew that he was capable of doing so, but my mind always got in the way of accepting it.

Then, one day, just as I was coming to grips with the fact that my vibrant, loving father would soon die, God interrupted the course of nature. My father's brain tumor, which the doctors just months before had called "highly malignant, fast-growing, and inoperable," suddenly disappeared.

My father's neurosurgeon, an atheist, didn't hesitate to call it a miracle. But I didn't dare to begin to hope, even though all of the tests that confirmed the original diagnosis now confirmed the absence of the tumor. It hadn't just stopped growing. It had shrunk to the point that it was barely detectable. I wanted to be happy, but mostly I was shocked.

I had been taught to "pray in faith, believing" (Matthew 21:22 KJV), but I recognized that mostly I prayed in fear, hoping. Sometimes I prayed in despair, doubting. During those times, the only prayer that came to me was "Help thou mine unbelief" (Mark 9:24 KJV). I despaired in my limited ability to look directly at glory without turning away.

My father's miracle gave us unexpected extra months to be with him. But then another tumor appeared, and this one didn't go away. Eventually my father died, two-and-a-half years after the original prognosis that gave him fewer than three months to live.

Yet despite our grief, my family knew that we had been witnesses to a miracle. We probably understand miracles less now than we did before my father's healing. But we do know that they happen.

There are many examples of miracles in the Bible, and I read them now with new understanding. People seemed to accept blind men suddenly seeing or the dead coming back to life. But as I read those accounts now, I put myself into the situations and always my reaction is the same: I would be one of the doubters, not one of those who so easily believed.

Jesus upset the natural order of things in a profound way. He didn't do the predictable or the understandable. Witnessing a miracle doesn't make it any more understandable. But I have witnessed one, and I know that miracles don't just change the course of events, they change hearts....

Dale Hanson Bourke is the publisher of Religious News Service, Washington, D. C., a syndicated columnist, and author of several books.

THE HOUSE CHURCH IN CHINA

by Carl Lawrence

To ask a participant in the house church in China whether or not he is experiencing things that might be classified as unusual for believers is to invite a quizzical reply: "I don't know what you mean by 'unusual.'"

"Well, you know, things a little strange…things that don't happen every day."

"You mean miracles?"

"Yes…yes, I guess that is what I mean. Yes, that's what I mean…miracles."

"You mean healings?"

"Yes, healings…you know, like Mr. Huang."

Mr. Huang was a worshiper of Buddha. His health began to deteriorate until he could not keep any food in his stomach at all. After a thorough examination, the doctor diagnosed his case: "You have cancer of the liver and are at the terminal stage. There is nothing we can do for you."

Mr. Huang returned to a small town near his native village to await the inevitable. While there, he heard about a doctor in the town and decided to get a second opinion or perhaps obtain some medicine that could prolong his life. This doctor was a Christian. Later, this doctor would accompany Mr. Huang as he gave his testimony. The Christian doctor confirmed the first diagnosis as cancer of the liver in an incurable, terminal stage.

The Christian doctor told the man that there was no medicine that could prolong his life, but that if the man would believe in Jesus Christ, he could have eternal life. He carefully explained the gospel to the man and urged him to believe on the Lord Jesus Christ. The doctor also explained that Jesus was the Lord and had the power to heal any sickness if it was His will. "But whether Jesus heals you or not is not important," the doctor said. "What is important is that you have eternal life."

"I want to believe in Jesus," Mr. Huang said. The doctor called in another Christian man, and the three of them knelt in his office as Mr. Huang became a new person in Jesus Christ.

Returning to his home, he told his wife of his faith in Jesus Christ and asked her to remove all the idols from the house and burn them. She did as she was told. She knew her husband's condition was hopeless. From then on, Mr. Huang's condition deteriorated rapidly. Every night, he and his wife knelt and prayed together. He thanked the Lord that whatever happened to him physically, he now had eternal life. He was gripped by terrible pain. His wife fixed some herbal and chicken soup, but it only made matters worse. In fact, over the next weeks, he became so weak that the family began preparations for his funeral. The coffin was purchased and the grave dug on the hillside.

One night a man in a white robe appeared to him in his sleep. The man was holding a knife. Not knowing what he intended to do, Mr. Huang struggled with the man in white, but the man prevailed and touched Mr. Huang with the knife. He awoke the next morning at 8 o'clock and was hungry for the first time in many days. After eating a nourishing bowl of egg-drop soup, he fell asleep. When he awakened, he saw two men in white robes standing by his bed.

"You have been healed," they said. He reached down and found all the pain and swelling gone. Being extremely hungry, he ate a hearty meal. When his brother came to pay him a last visit, he was amazed to see him sitting up and strong. He told his brother that Jesus had touched him during the night and he was completely healed.

This event can be attested to by several of his co-workers and a Christian medical doctor who has witnessed patients being divinely healed.

Carl Lawrence is a Gold Medallion-winning author, served twenty years with the Far East Broadcasting Company, and is the author of The Coming Influence of China.

Miracles of

CHANGED

LIVES

This is real faith: believing and acting obediently

regardless of circumstances or contrary evidence.

After all, if faith depended on visible evidence, it wouldn't be faith.

Charles Colson

Miracles of
CHANGED
LIVES

I don't know about you, but when I make up my mind about something I like to *keep* it made up. You may call me stubborn. I like to think of myself as "resolute." Either way, it's difficult for me to change my position once I've chosen one. But when I realize that I'm misinformed, w*rong* about something, I make myself reconsider my stand. The one thing I hate worse than being wishy-washy is being foolish.

Early on in my life, I made up my mind about God. I could have taken one of only three positions. That of:

- atheists (those who claim there is no God)
- agnostics (those who say, "If there is a God you can't know it"), or
- theists (those who believe there is a God and you can know him).

Early on, I was probably an agnostic. But along the way, I changed my mind about the claims of Jesus Christ. Today, I fall into category three.

Now, my conversion wasn't triggered by the occurrence of miraculous events (although there are those who might argue that my conversion itself was a miracle!). But for millions of men, women, and children, a miracle was the catalyst for their spiritual decision. These are the stories of what happened to some of them—and how their lives were changed forever.

WE WERE IN ROW TWENTY-SIX

by John Aker

One day in November, on my way to a special meeting at Trinity College in Deerfield, Illinois, I got on a flight from Newark International Airport to Chicago's O'Hare.

As I boarded the DC-10, the emptiness of the flight surprised me. Many times I had traveled on it and found the plane quite full. Despite that, the computer had decreed that I should sit beside a fellow traveler. He had the window seat…I had the aisle one. Looking across the five seats in the middle, I intended to lift the arms of all of them and stretch out. In the meantime, though, I would be just a bit sociable—after all, I was a minister. So I began to speak to him.

His name was Dick, and I quickly found out we had much in common. We both studied at the Army Intelligence School, had married women in the army intelligence, and had three children. That's where our commonalities ended.

Dick told me he had been to New York City's Sloan Kettering Cancer Institute. He had come to an agreement with his doctor that there would be no more chemotherapy or radiation treatment. He just wanted to go home, back to Beatrice, Nebraska, where he worked as comptroller at the Lutheran

Hospital. He wanted to live full throttle before his kids. The doctors told him it would be just a few months—six, eight, maybe ten...but not many.

After a while, Dick began to turn toward me. Until then I had seen only the right side of his face—so normal...so whole. Little by little, the left side came into view, and I saw the ravages of the disease: basal cell carcinoma—"skin cancer."

For the first time I saw the way the tongue lay in the mouth...how the teeth bit up and down into the jaw...the way the eye socket is formed and holds the eye in place—because all the skin was gone. It was one raw, open wound.

Here was a man facing certain death, short of a special miracle by God. Yet his greatest concern was for the three children he would have to leave behind. He told me he had been an only child, as was his wife. A few months earlier, she had fallen on the basement steps and died. Now as he knew he would have to leave his children, only his aged parents remained to care for them. They lived in New Jersey and had never known anything outside that state...and his children knew only Beatrice, Nebraska.

At that point I looked at Dick and asked, "Do you mind if I tell you why I am not an intelligence agent anymore? Can I tell you about something that really changed my life?"

Dick nodded, and I took a napkin left over from breakfast and sketched out my version of "The Four Spiritual Laws." When I came to the end of that simple presentation, the stewardess interrupted our conversation: "We are now preparing for final descent into Chicago's O'Hare Airport."

"Dick, can't you trust Jesus Christ for your future...what lies beyond the grave for you and your children? Can you look to the One who left His own grave behind and believe that He holds some hope for you and for the care of your children?"

Like a dying man, Dick clutched my hand and said, "Pray with me." Right then, at about ten thousand feet above Chicago, Dick Wieger gave his heart to Jesus Christ.

We had just concluded the sinner's prayer when the big plane touched down. Following Dick along the ramp and into the lobby, I thought for a moment about my wife and children. As we shook hands, I saw Dick waving—only the right side of his face, fully alive and warmly smiling—at me. I reflected on the graciousness of God, who took someone like me and allowed me to share in His work, the miracle of taking people from death to life.

Had the story ended there, it would have remained merely special....

The first Sunday of May of the following year, I was on the East Coast, preaching. Sunday seemed longer than before. I got on the same flight to O'Hare and felt tired, very tired. But I was going home. The computer had graciously reserved me a seat next to a nice older woman. I figured she wouldn't mind if I sat back, buckled up, and went to sleep, so I did just that. But shortly after breakfast I woke up and realized I'd not taken time to invest in her life or allowed her to share her life with me.

I began by asking if she lived in Chicago. No, she told me. She was on her way to a little town in Nebraska. I asked her which one.

"Oh, you've probably never heard of it," she warned me.

"Try me."

"Beatrice."

"I know Beatrice," I responded. "I know the comptroller of the hospital there."

She looked at me in total surprise. "You know Dick?"

"Yes, I sat with him on this very plane last November...this same flight."

"You must be John."

"How could you know that?"

She simply replied, "I'm Dick's mother."

June Wieger went on to tell me how Dick had begun to walk in the decision he made for Christ. He was reading the Bible, getting together with his pastor, praying, concerned about Bible study. Having the assurance that Dick was taking his final steps with his Master, with her Lord, meant something special to June.

At this point the stewardess announced, "We're now preparing for final descent into Chicago's O'Hare Airport."

Our eyes locked as I said, "You know, June, this is when I prayed with Dick."

Just as her son had done, she took my hand and asked, "Would you pray with me?" And I did.

The plane pulled up to the ramp just as we finished. June looked at me and commented, "You know, I'm so encouraged."

"Encouraged?" I replied. "I feel inspired! To think that one casual meeting with Dick, and he's following through on that decision...that he's been concerned about a deeper relationship with his Lord...to see the way God takes our lives, causes them to intersect, and puts all the pieces together so perfectly...just the way He arranged for us to sit together. People would never believe it."

She looked at me and said, "You know, this wasn't my seat." We were in row twenty-six, seats A and B. "I was assigned to row twenty-four, and just before you came on board, a woman asked me to change with her."

John Aker is a minister and author.

Jesus...and Jim

by J. Sidlow Baxter

ome time ago, in a southern English town, the clergyman of
an Anglican church happened to be looking out through his
vicarage window when he saw a rather rough-looking
workman stroll past the main door of the church, where he
halted rather furtively, and then entered. The next day the clergyman noticed the same thing; and again a couple of days later,
always about the same time, twelve-thirty noon. His suspicions
became aroused, so he set the verger to spy.

This is what the verger saw: the man entered, stuffed his
cap into his jacket pocket, and walked down the main aisle, to
the rail before the communion table. There, with bowed head,
he stood in silence. Then, putting his hands on the communion rail, and looking over toward the communion table, he
said in a low voice, "Jesus...it's Jim."

Some days later there was a nasty accident in town, and Jim
was carried to the local hospital. He was put in a men's ward
which at that time was filled with the roughest mixture of men
ever admitted. Such was their coarseness and crude ungrateful-
ness that more than one of the nurses had shed tears. However,
after Jim had been there a few days there was a marked change;

and after two or three days more it was such that the sister and nurses simply could not conceal their happy surprise.

One morning, just as the sister entered to start her round of the beds, the men were all enjoying a good-natured laugh at something. She could not help asking the first man what it was which made such a change in them all. He replied: "Oh, it's that chap in the fifth bed. They call 'im Jim."

So when the screen was round Jim's bed, she said to him: "Jim, you've made a wonderful change in this ward. Tell me how you've done it."

With a tear glistening in his eyes, Jim replied: "Well, sister, I'm not sure you'd understand if I told you. But somehow, every day, just about twelve-thirty, I see Jesus coming toward the end o' my bed. He stands there for a minute; then he just puts His hands on the bed rail, an' leans over and says: 'Jim…it's Jesus.'"

J. Sidlow Baxter is a Scottish preacher, lecturer, and author.

PROJECT PEARL

by Jeff Taylor

n 1981 Pastor Chen was arrested for his part in delivering more than one million Bibles to Swatow, on the south China coast. Four interrogators were flown in from Beijing but still Pastor Chen refused to release the names of those who met in a secret house church or those who helped deliver Bibles under the code name "Project Pearl."

"This is your last chance, Chen!" the first investigator threatened. "We know you were a key organizer of this 'Project Pearl.' We know you are a key leader of the illegal house churches. We know you live in Swatow where the Bibles were delivered. You had better talk now, or your situation will be worse than you ever imagined!"

Chen still refused to answer any more questions. He knew that to speak was futile. It was obvious the investigators had already made up their minds. They needed names, more names, in order to piece together how the project began. Yet the interrogators couldn't help but be impressed by the serenity that had come over Chen, even as their questioning became increasingly harsh. Chen had gone through similar things during the

Cultural Revolution. He knew how to handle this kind of inter-rogation—so he shut his eyes and prayed.

Exasperated, the investigators took Chen into a courtyard in the prison and made him stand on a tall wooden box. They knew beatings wouldn't help. He was a frail man, but quite unafraid of dying.

A rope was put around his neck and tightened. The rope was fixed on a wooden beam above him. The box he was standing on was about four feet high, and very narrow.

Angrily, the first investigator said, "We have given up on you. The moment you sway, or when your legs collapse from tiredness, you will hang yourself. That is the penalty for your stubbornness!"

The two investigators were assigned to watch Chen's last moments. As he looked down on them, he observed that they took hardly any notice of him. Bored, they played games. At that moment, Chen felt a surge of power in his body. *I feel just like Jesus on the cross*, he thought. *He must have looked down and felt the same when he saw the soldiers casting lots for his clothes, utterly indifferent to his agonies.*

Knowing his end was not far away, Chen began to witness to the two policemen.

"Have you ever heard of Jesus?" he asked.

"Quiet, Christian!" spat the first investigator. "We don't want to hear about your Jesus! It's just an old myth."

"Oh no," Chen continued, "Jesus is no myth. He loves you. And He loves me. He came to earth as a man to die for your sins and my sins; for the sins of the whole world. Then He rose from death on the third day. Because He's my savior, I know I will go to heaven. I'm not afraid to die."

The second investigator said, "Old man, when I get to be seventy and look as unhealthy as you, I won't be afraid of death either!" The two investigators laughed.

The long hours soon became days, yet Chen had to remain still. His body cried for sleep, but he could not give in to his feelings. His legs developed terrible cramps, and, in shaking them, he nearly hanged himself. Soon he felt nothing in his legs, even though they had swollen to twice their normal size. His only relief was the rain. He stuck his thickened tongue out to gain a few drops of moisture. The rain also helped by washing his filthy body.

Five days passed. Six. Seven. Still Chen had not toppled over and died. Eight. Nine days. The word was going around the prison. Surely no man could survive that long. He had been standing all that time. No food. No water. No rest. It was impossible for him to still be alive.

Ten days passed. Eleven, and then twelve. On the thirteenth day, a huge thunderstorm rolled in. The sky went black, and the rain poured down. His resistance was over. Through his delirium he heard the crash of thunder, saw a flash of lightning, as he fell forward. The rope tightened. Oblivion.

Was that water Chen felt someone splashing over his cracked and puffy lips? Someone else seemed to be rubbing his wrists. His legs had been propped up on a chair and he felt the blood pumping back into his body and arms. He could do nothing but cry from the pain.

He soon became aware of who it was who was working on him. It was the two investigators. Why were they suddenly so interested in reviving an old man they had mocked, an old man who they couldn't care less whether he lived or died? Why had he not been strangled by the rope? The two investigators began to shake him urgently.

"Quick! Don't die, please! You've got to wake up! Please don't die!" pleaded the second investigator.

Weakly, Chen asked, "Why? What's happening? Where am I?"

"Please, we want to know how to know your savior, Jesus," the first investigator said. Chen could feel him trembling.

"I don't understand," Chen said. "Why?"

"Because He saved you," the second investigator explained. "A flash of lightning cut the rope above your head just as you fell. Don't try to tell us it was coincidence!"

Both of the investigators came to faith in Christ that day. The tears of all three men mingled with the pouring rain as the investigators repented of their sins.

Pastor Chen was later released, more out of indecision than anything else. The story had spread around the prison, and he was held in some awe. None of the other investigators had the courage to interrogate him again...so they let him go.

Jeff Tayler is the managing editor of Compass Direct *and writes for* Open Doors, *a ministry that delivers Bibles in areas where the Church is persecuted.*

UNCLE ROGER

by Rebecca Manley Pippert

N ever was the awesome importance of what we decide more poignant to me than in the recent death of my Uncle Roger, the kindest, warmest man I have ever known. A marathon runner and the picture of health, he was abruptly diagnosed as having terminal lung cancer at the age of sixty. We hoped against hope that the chemotherapy would prove effective, but the cancer spread too rapidly. One morning I received a call from my mother telling me he was not expected to live through the day. Only one thought plagued me: though he was a wonderful man, by his own admission he had not put his faith in God. Now it seemed too late. I could not get home to Illinois soon enough to talk to him, and he was lapsing into a semi-coma. But the thought that I would not share eternity with him in God's presence was more than I could bear. There was only one thing to do—pray.

I called one of my best friends, with whom I pray frequently. She is one of the most spiritually sensitive people I have ever known, but what she told me left me stunned. She said she had awakened in the middle of the night feeling burdened to pray for someone in danger. But she did not know who or what was involved. She went downstairs and began to pray and read the Bible. As she prayed, she felt the Spirit of God, along with the passages she was reading, confirm that someone was dying and she was supposed to pray for that person. She wanted to go back to bed, but could not shake the desperate sense of need. Again she got out of bed and went back downstairs to pray until dawn. Then came my call a few hours later.

So my friend and I prayed. We prayed that God would not let Roger die before he had clearly heard the message of the gospel, and that he would receive it and believe. Throughout the day I was in touch with my family. The medical news was always the same. He was still in a semi-coma, eyes closed, saying nothing. My handsome, always smiling, athletic six-foot uncle had become in only four months emaciated, bald, and looking like an old man. He was breathing through a mask and his doctors felt he could not last the day. I did nothing but pray and fast. My friend did the same. We begged God to let him live, so he could hear and believe. But who would tell him? What possible good would it do with him in a coma?

That night my mother called and said, "No one can believe it, but Roger was suddenly alert, eyes opened and talking. Now the doctors wonder if he might have more like a month or more to live." I began planning my trip home but continued to pray that God would send a messenger to Roger. But his alertness lasted only that evening—thankfully giving him time to talk to his wife and children. Then he sank again. It was now very clear that death was not far away.

The next day he stayed in his semi-coma state, totally unable to communicate. My friend and I prayed and fasted all of that day too. I walked through the park, asking God for the same thing we had ever since we received the news—for Roger to revive long enough to hear the message and for someone on the spot to take the initiative to talk to him. Then something remarkable happened. A hometown doctor, Roger Weiss, who was a friend of the family and a Christian, felt an inner urge to go to the hospital and share the gospel with Uncle Roger. When he called he was told that a visit was probably not possible because Roger's condition had deteriorated, but throughout the day Dr. Weiss could not shake the urge. He became convinced that God was leading him to go, even though Uncle Roger was in a coma. Finally he called the family and said, "I'm coming anyway. I'll be there in ten minutes." At 4:55 Roger suddenly woke up out of the coma and smiled, and the first thing he did was ask about his mother, concerned about her. He was totally alert. Nurses began flying around. No one could believe he had revived again. At 5:00 P.M. in walked Dr. Weiss.

For the next twenty minutes Dr. Weiss talked with Uncle Roger. He told him, "You are one of the finest men I have known. But have you done things wrong in your life, Roger? Things you truly regret?"

"Oh yes, so many," Roger said.

"Jesus came to forgive us the wrong we've done," the doctor said. "He died to put it right because, as good as you are, being good isn't enough. We have all fallen short of God's standards. We are all guilty of not making Him the center of our lives. Jesus is here. He wants to reach out to you, even in this last hour. He longs to forgive you. But you are the only one who can make that decision. The ball is in your court. So you understand everything I am saying?"

"Yes," answered Roger. "I just wish you had told me this sooner." There was a moment of silence and Roger said, "I'm not ready yet. I need more time to think about it."

Dr. Weiss answered warmly, "God loves you so much, He

may give you more time. I pray that He will." That was the last time he saw Roger alive.

While Roger was still alert the family was able to say good-bye. A few hours later, my mother, Uncle Roger's only sibling, came in. "Do you remember when Dr. Weiss was here and what he talked to you about?" she asked. "Yes, I do," he responded. "I just want you to know that I can't bear the thought of spending eternity without you either," she said. He smiled and thanked her saying, "I'm still thinking about it."

Shortly after that he went back into a semi-coma. His daughter and wife stayed by his side throughout the night. He spoke incoherently reliving the past, as his mind wandered freely.

My aunt slipped out of the room for a few minutes. Suddenly Roger looked directly at his daughter, Meg, and said in a clear voice and with clear eyes, "Meg, did you see him when he came to visit me?"

"Did I see whom, Daddy?"

"He came to me. He came right here to my bed. He spoke to me. Father."

Since they were the first coherent words he had spoken for hours, and since no one in the family referred to the deceased grandfather as anything but Daddy, Meg felt something extraordinary had happened.

"Dad," she said. "I'm not sure what you mean. But I have something very important to tell you. It means everything to me. Do you remember what Dr. Weiss and Sue talked to you about?"

"Yes, I do," he answered.

"Dad, I hope you will choose to give your life to Jesus."

He did not speak for a moment. Then he said, "I already have, Meg. I asked him. I said yes."

Those were the last coherent words Roger ever spoke. He slipped into a deep coma. The next morning my mom came to stay with him. She held the hand of her only brother and eased him into death. "Jesus is here, Roger. He loves you so. He'll take you home now. You've suffered enough. Just put your hand in his. It's time to go home." And he died.

As Roger died, I was in an airplane on my way to Champaign. The one thing I prayed for, aside from his salvation, was that, if he had decided to choose God, we would know. The day of my flight I changed my reservations three times. I felt as if I were in a total fog. When I had to change planes in Ohio, I called home to see if there was any news. Mother told me that Uncle Roger had just died, but she told me that he had died a believer.

Standing in front of the pay telephone with tears streaming down my face, I can safely say that I have never worshiped God in more purity and fullness than I did at that moment. To think that a dying man could say, "I need more time," and God would give it to him. He brings a doctor in from out of nowhere, wakes Roger up from a coma, all because he loves him, and because the choice is that critical. Dr. Weiss said it was a celestial commando raid to reach Roger. As I boarded the plane on that last leg of the flight to Champaign, I thought if only I could share this moment and tell someone who means something to me what God has done. I fumbled for my ticket with tear-stained eyes to see my seat assignment. I sat down, sighed deeply, and looked over at the passenger in the seat next to me. There to my utter astonishment was my brother, Bob, on his way from Miami to Champaign. That we would end up next to each other on a plane in Ohio is something only God could have arranged.

This deeply personal story reveals so much of what God is

like. It also reveals the means of grace that God used to reach my uncle: the Spirit of God that awakened my friend to pray, who moved Dr. Weiss to talk to Roger even though it seemed absurd under the circumstances. It also reveals the critical importance of the will, how terribly important our decision of faith is. But most of all it's a story about a God who loves us, and who reaches out to us.

Rebecca Manley Pippert is a best-selling author, popular speaker, and leader with Intervarsity Christian Fellowship.

LET'S SING IT!

by Charles Colson

Easter weekend at Walla Walla ended with a fitting postscript, yet another sign of the Kingdom at work. Fred, a young man with a heroin habit and a robbery record, had done time at Walla Walla. The family of one of his robbery victims had prayed for him for years, visited him in prison, and eventually led him to Christ. During a subsequent parole hearing, Fred had confessed to additional crimes of which he had not been convicted, explaining to the startled parole board that as a Christian, he felt he could not do otherwise.

Fred's original conviction was overturned; he was released from prison and began to rebuild his life. He became active in a local church and got involved in a Christian ex-prisoner fellowship while awaiting his retrial.

As it happened, Fred's case was scheduled to be heard on Easter Monday. The Seattle Superior Court was filled with friends, family, and supporters who had already testified on his behalf. Fred had freely confessed his guilt; and now he told Judge Francis Holman that he was prepared to accept whatever punishment the judge deemed appropriate. For in any event, said Fred, "I am ready to go back to prison and serve Jesus Christ in there."

The judge leaned back in his tall leather chair and ticked off a long list of possible sentences. There was an awkward, drawn-out silence.

Then Judge Holman pounded his gavel. Ten years on each count of robbery—suspended. Fred would be free on probation, provided he would continue in a drug-treatment program and make restitution to his victims at 150 percent of their loss, or $2,200. He looked down at Fred again, his face still solemn: "We send you on your way with best wishes."

For a moment no one moved. Then Fred's pastor jumped to his feet and gestured to the packed courtroom. "Let's sing it!" he shouted.

A reporter for the *Seattle Times* captured what came next: "Everyone stood up, little old ladies in spring dresses, ex-cons, girls in jeans, prison guards—and they began to sing: 'Praise God from whom all blessings flow....'"

Charles Colson is founder and chairman of Prison Fellowship Ministries.

A PLACE OF PEACE

by Jeff Taylor

Colombia is considered one of the most violent countries in the world. Many areas of the country are controlled by either drug cartels, subversive guerrilla groups, or a combination of the two.

As these illegal groups battle for control with the government's military, the church is often caught in the crossfire. Since the Christians refuse to take sides, they are considered the enemy by all.

In a very remote area of Colombia stands a small church. It has the largest congregation in the entire region...with fifteen members. But this congregation of fifteen members is a church of much prayer.

Recently, the church was meeting for prayer. They met in an old wooden shack that looked as if it should have been condemned long ago. No windows. No doors. No electricity. And a dirt floor.

Dusk was fast approaching as the fellowship prayed fervently for each other and for the violence that was rampant. They prayed for peace in their region. And they prayed for peace in the hearts of those who sought to use violence to accomplish their purposes.

Passing unnoticed on the north side of the church was a small patrol of guerrilla soldiers who controlled this area. They were the ones to grant or deny permission for any meetings. They even collected the taxes.

At the same time these guerrilla soldiers were passing by, an army patrol began to approach the church from the south. They were on a reconnaissance mission into the area in hopes of eventually taking control.

And this small congregation was right in the middle.

When the military saw the Christians in the shack, they assumed it was a group of subversives meeting to plan their strategy. When the guerrillas saw the Christians, they mistakenly identified them as a military patrol plotting to retake the area. They knew they had not approved any meeting.

Simultaneously both groups began to fire on this congregation.

For several minutes mortars and shots rained on the rickety old building. The firepower used was so immense for this small building that the smoke and dust seemed to totally obscure what was happening. Finally, the calls to cease firing were heard. Several more minutes passed as the smoke cleared.

To every soldier's amazement, the firing had had no effect. None of the shots had penetrated the building. The blasts had not dislodged a single plank!

Both patrols immediately left the area to regroup. There was no explanation for what happened.

Late the following day, the small guerrilla patrol carefully and quietly approached the church where the congregation was meeting again for prayer. At their commander's signal, they burst in, aiming their rifles at the Christians.

"Who are you?!" demanded the guerrilla commander. "What are you doing here?"

"We are Christians, and we meet here daily for prayer," one of them answered. "You are welcome to join us. But you will have to put down your rifles. There is no need for them here."

The guerrillas were not ready to stay. They knew something unexplainable had taken place. Here was a power they had not encountered before. So as they began to file out of the church, the commander turned and left the Christians with a request: "We would be grateful if you would please pray for us."

"We *have* been praying for you," one of the Christians said, "and we will continue to do so."

This faithful congregation was not surprised when, only a few days later, the *same scene* was repeated—only this time it was with the military patrol. They, too, asked for prayer.

An Open Doors team member who recently visited the area related how the church is now a city of refuge for the Lord in this violence-prone area. The Christians are not harmed now by either group. It is a place of peace in the midst of war.

Jeff Tayler is the managing editor of Compass Direct *and writes for Open Doors, a ministry that delivers Bibles in areas where the Church is persecuted.*

The Two

GREATEST

MIRACLES

General belief in God is one thing, but it is quite another matter

to embrace the miracles of the Virgin Birth, His rising from the dead,

and His own ascension from the grave.

Yet it is "irrational" to reject miracles a priori.

Antonin Scalia

Supreme Court Justice

The Two
GREATEST
MIRACLES

Whatʼs your favorite miracle so far? Perhaps itʼs the chance meeting on a subway that resulted in the reunion of a man and wife tragically separated by war. Maybe you are drawn to the story of a tow truck that got two boys home safely and then disappeared, leaving no tire tracks in the snow. Or maybe you loved hearing about one little girl in the tropics with the innocent faith it takes to ask God for a hot water bottle—and a doll for a sad friend.

There's no question about it: God truly does work in beautiful, wonderful ways. But, as incredible—as unbelievably glorious—as these miracles are, you need to know this amazing truth:

God saved the two greatest miracles of all for *you*.

Sit back now and prepare to receive what God is about to reveal to you. No matter how many times you hear the stories, they cannot grow old…the message within them simply makes your life richer as your understanding grows.

These are *your* miracles. Embrace them. Feel their power. Revel in their beauty. But most of all, open your heart now to the one who gives them.

He is *your* Miracle Maker.

God Came

by Joni Eareckson Tada

What might have been God's greatest miracle? There are certainly enough from which to choose.

Think of the Old Testament miracles like the destruction of Sodom and Gomorrah, the parting of the Red Sea, or the day the sun stood still at the prayer of Joshua. How about creation itself? A universe leaping into existence at the merest word of the mighty Creator!

Over in the New Testament you could include Jesus turning water into wine, walking on water, quieting an angry sea, or raising the dead.

The list is long, the examples are many, and I'm sure the debate could go on indefinitely. But, let me propose a miracle in a class by itself....

Consider the fullness of God—the God who set suns and stars in motion, ladled out seas, dreamed up time and space, and formed you and me in the womb. Then imagine this same God coming to earth as an infant! God—the very essence of love and holiness, justice and mercy— entering history *in baby flesh*. The very voice which once spoke creation into being, now crying for mother's milk. The eyes of the Ancient of Days that roamed to and fro throughout the galaxies, now new, blurred, and teary. *God*...with little pink hands. Little nubby feet. Soft, silky hair and fresh, dewy skin.

What miracle can compare with that?

Shaking his head in wonder, the apostle writes of the One...

Who, being in very nature God,
did not consider equality with God something to be grasped,
but made himself nothing,
taking the very nature of a servant,
being made in human likeness.
And being found in appearance as a man,
he humbled himself....

PHILIPPIANS 2:6–8

When you think about it, incarnation is such a mind-staggering miracle it makes the rest of those miracles seem almost secondary.

If we can believe that God came in the flesh, then all other miracles are simple. Changing water into wine? Nothing to it. Opening blind eyes? Child's play! Raising men from the dead? No great matter for the Lord Jesus. The biggest miracle of all, the miracle of His birth, makes all the other stunning things that happened seem minor. Almost simple.

Joni Eareckson Tada is director of "Joni and Friends," a ministry to the disabled, and author of best-selling books including Secret Strength *and* Glorious Intruder.

EXTRAORDINARY MOMENT

by Max Lucado

Jesus wasn't displaying His power.

It was an ordinary week...packed with kids being dressed by impatient moms and dads hustling off to work...of dishes being washed and floors swept.

Nature gave no clue that this week was different from any of the thousands before it or after. The sun took its habitual route, clouds puffed through the Judean sky, the grass was green, cattails danced in the wind.

Nature would groan before Sunday. Rocks would tumble and the sky would put on a black robe. You wouldn't know that by looking at Monday, Tuesday, Wednesday, or Thursday. The week told no secrets.

The people gave no clue either. For most it was a weekend of festivities arriving. Food to be bought, houses cleaned. Faces gave no forecast of the extraordinary—for they knew of none.

One would think the disciples would suspect something; they don't.... The only thing they know for sure is that his eyes seem more focused—he seems determined...about what they aren't sure.

And most importantly, Jesus gives no clue.

You'd think the heavens would be opened, trumpets sounding, angels summoning all the people of the world to Jerusalem to witness the event. You'd think that God himself would descend to bless his Son.

But he doesn't. He leaves the extraordinary moment draped in the ordinary. A predictable week. A week of tasks, meals, and crying babies.

A week which may be a lot like yours.

For the people of Jerusalem the edge of history's most remarkable hour was one of history's unremarkable weeks. God is in their city and most miss him.

Jesus could have used the spectacular to get their attention—stun them with a loop-a-dee-loop or a double back-flip off the temple. When they demanded "Crucify him!" why didn't he make their noses grow? Why is the miraculous part of Christ quiet this week? Why doesn't he do something spectacular?

No angelic shield protected his back from the whip. No holy helmet shielded his brow from the thorny crown. God crawled neck deep into the mire of humanity, plunged into the darkest cave of death, and emerged—alive.

Even when he came out, he didn't show off. He just walked out. Mary thought he was a gardener.

God calls us in the real world. He doesn't communicate by performing tricks. God's not a trickster, a genie, a magician, or a good luck charm. He is the creator of the universe, right here in the thick of your day-to-day world speaking to you through cooing babies and hungry bellies.

Don't miss the impossible by looking for the incredible.... Listen for him amidst the ordinary.

In the final week those who demanded miracles got none and missed the one. They missed the moment in which a grave for the dead became the throne of a king.

Max Lucado is a pastor, and author of several best-selling books including And the Angels Were Silent *and* No Wonder They Call Him the Savior.

A Final

WORD

Faith does not spring from the miracle,

but the miracle from faith.

Fyodor Dostoevsky

A Final
WORD

The mind or the soul? Facts or faith? It's likely that at one time or another, you've felt pressured to align yourself with one side or the other. Let's face it, science and religion have been at each other's throats for centuries over subjects of the supernatural, and that includes the topic of miracles.

Some experts claim to have proven the scientific impossibility of miracles. (Since an explanation of miracles doesn't fit the traditional structure of scientific truth, it is reasoned that they simply cannot occur.) At the same time, vast numbers of miraculous occurrences are reported every day, by men, women, and children from every possible cultural, educational, and professional background.

So what is the truth? Whom can you believe?

Like you, I wouldn't want to choose between science and religion. Thankfully, I've found a third option—one in which there doesn't have to be a battle—and that option is this: perhaps the existence of miracles is not a question best posed to the scientific community at all.

Let me explain. You see, when exploring the scientific validity of miracles, it's important to note that miracles are, by their very nature, unique, unpredictable, unexpected historical events. Science, on the other hand, is defined as "a branch of knowledge or study dealing with a body of facts or truths systematically arranged and showing the operation of general laws."[1] As you've already discovered, there is nothing systematic about a miracle. They do not operate by a series of laws. They simply *happen*. Since there is no way to predict their occurrence, there is no way to prove their existence. The scientific community is not positioned to give judgment about such rare and "nonscientific" events.

So where do we find answers, if not within the world of science? In the absence of measurable, provable explanations, we turn to the spiritual realm. Here, at last, we find a place for miracles. Here, there is room to believe that God the creator, who outfitted the world with physical laws, might intervene in his orderly system. Here, a miracle is still considered unusual. Yet under this paradigm, miracles can also be viewed as unique demonstrations of God's ongoing power to sustain his creation and to fulfill his purpose.

As he works to control his creation, God acts both continuously and freely. Such continuous behavior can be observed within "the operation of general laws" known to science. At rare times, however, in accordance with his specific goals, God *does* act freely. The result is miracles.

It doesn't take long to find proof that miracles *do* happen. The stories in this book—biblical and historical accounts, reports by friends and acquaintances, and our own, personal experiences—all provide evidence of this fact. The question remaining, then, is, *why* do they occur?

[1] Webster's College Dictionary

By now, I hope the reason is clear. They happen not because of some arbitrary violation of natural law. They happen because we have a freely creative and loving God who wants to make himself known. To me. And to you.

Do you know him? Do you want to know him better? You can, you know. Such a blessing is more than any one of us deserves. It's unexpected. It's undeserved. Yet it is very, very real.

And isn't that just like a miracle?

NOTES

If you would like to contribute stories for a
possible second edition of
UNSOLVED MIRACLES
please send them to the following address:

John Van Diest
Multnomah Publishers, Inc.
P.O. Box 1720
Sisters, OR 97759

For each story, please give the author's name, and the original
source of the story if it was previously published. Also, please
include your name, address, and phone number.
We will not be able to contact everyone who submits a story,
but we will notify you if the story you submit is used.
Manuscripts and photocopies cannot be returned.

We hope these stories have strengthened your faith and
inspired you.

Hundreds of books were researched for this collection and numerous submitted stories were reviewed. Reasonable care has been taken to trace original ownership, and when necessary, obtain permission to reprint. If we have overlooked giving proper credit to anyone, please contact Multnomah Publishers, Inc., Post Office Box 1720, Sisters, Oregon 97759. Corrections will be made prior to additional printings.

Notes and acknowledgments are listed by story title in the order they appear in each section of the book. For permission to reprint copyrighted material, grateful acknowledgment is made to the authors and publishers.

MIRACLES OF DESTINY

"It Happened on the Brooklyn Subway" by Paul Deutschman. Published in *Reader's Digest*, May 1949, © 1949 by Paul Deutschman. Reprinted by permission of Regina Ryan Publishing Enterprises, Inc, 251 Central park West, New York, NY 10024, and by the Reader's Digest Association, Inc.

"The Bullet" by Doris Sanford, Milwaukie, OR, © 1997. Used by permission.

"The Gold and Ivory Tablecloth" by Howard C. Schade. Reprinted with permission from the December, 1954 *Reader's Digest*, © 1966 by the Reader's Digest Association, Inc.

"Divine Honeymoon" by James Dobson from *When God Doesn't Make Sense* (Tyndale House Publishers, Inc, Wheaton, IL, © 1993). Used by permission. All rights reserved.

"Rescue Fire" by Billy Graham from *Hope for the Troubled Heart* (Word, Inc, Dallas, TX, ©1991).

"Strange Angels" by Jan Winebrenner from *God, You, and That Man with Three Goats* by Dan and Vera Hillis, © 1995. Used by permission of Dr. and Mrs. Don Hillis, 3307 Thurman Ave., Roanoke, VA 24012. All rights retained.

"The Men with the Bibles" submitted by Joe Aldrich. Author and original source unknown.

"Miracle in the Details" by Jerry Jenkins, *Moody Magazine*, March/April 1996. Used by permission of the author.

MIRACLES OF PROVISION

"Guiding Signs" by Dawn Raffel. Original source unknown.

"A Small Girl's Prayer," by Helen Roseveare from *God, You, and That Man with Three Goats* by Dan and Vera Hillis, © 1995. Used by permission of Dr. and Mrs. Don Hillis, 3307 Thurman Ave., Roanoke, VA 24012. All rights retained. Story title in original publication is "A Hot Water Bottle."

"Tornado!" Joan Wester Anderson from the book *Where Angels Walk: True Stories of Heavenly Visitors*. ©1992 by Joan Wester Anderson. Published by Barton & Brett, Publishers, Inc. Reprinted by permission. Story title in original publication is "Companion Through the Storm."

"When the Rain Came" by Una Roberts Lawrence, adapted from *Gospel Gleaners*, vol. X, no. 1, part 1, Springfield, MO, January 3, 1937.

"Mary's Secret List" by Barb Marshall, Pickerington, OH, © 1997. Used by permission.

"Providence Spring" by J. C. Sills. Published in *Light and Life Evangel*, October 8, 1950.

"The Bridge That Wasn't There" by Howard Foltz. This article was taken from *Decision* magazine, October 1996, © 1996 Billy Graham Evangelistic Association. Used by permission. All rights reserved.

"An Unlikely Rain" by Doris Sanford, Milwaukie, OR, © 1997. Used by permission.

"Faith and Action" by Henry T. Blackaby and Claude V. King from *Experiencing God* (Broadman and Holman Publishers, Nashville, TN, © 1994). Used by permission. All rights reserved.

"My Encourager" by Kenneth Taylor from *My Life: A Guided Tour* (Tyndale House Publishers, Inc, Wheaton, IL, ©1991). Used by permission. All rights reserved.

"The Music Box" by Sherry Angel from "Believing in Miracles" in *Horizons Magazine*, May/June 1996.

"One Thousand Dollars Short" by Bernie May from from *God, You, and That Man with Three Goats* by Dan and Vera Hillis, © 1995. Used by permission of Dr. and Mrs. Don Hillis, 3307 Thurman Ave., Roanoke, VA 24012. All rights retained. Story title in original publication is "Putting Disjointed Events Together."

"Right on Top" by Mother Teresa from *In the Heart of the World* (New World Library, San Francisco, CA, © 1997). Used by permission.

MIRACLES AND ANGELS

"In a Moment of Time" by Hope MacDonald from *When Angels Appear* (Zondervan Publishing House, Grand Rapids, MI, ©1982). Used by permission of Zondervan Publishing House.

"Safely Home" by Joan Wester Anderson from the book *Where Angels Walk: True Stories of Heavenly Visitors*. ©1992 by Joan Wester Anderson. Published by Barton & Brett, Publishers, Inc. Reprinted by permission. Story title in original publication is "The Beginning."

"Marching Orders" by Corrie ten Boom from *Marching Orders for the End Battle* (Christian Literature Crusade, Fort Washington, PA ©1993).

"On a Winter Night" by Billy Graham from *Angels: God's Secret Agents* (Word, Inc, Dallas, TX, © 1975, 1986, 1994, 1995 by Billy Graham).

"Intervention on the Front Lines" by David Jeremiah from *What the Bible Says About Angels* (Multnomah Publishers, Inc, Sisters, OR, © 1996).

"Missed Overalls" by Sam Graham Humphreys, © 1997. Used by permission of the author. All rights retained.

"Large Fiery Figures" by David Jeremiah from *What the Bible Says About Angels* (Multnomah Publishers, Inc, Sisters, OR, © 1996).

"A Voice of Warning" by Hope MacDonald from *When Angels Appear* (Zondervan Publishing House, Grand Rapids, MI, © 1982). Used by permission of Zondervan Publishing House.

Through Gates of Splendor" by Olive Fleming Liefeld from *Unfolding Destinies* (Zondervan Publishing House, Grand Rapids, MI, © 1990). Used by permission of Zondervan Publishing House.

"Stranger at the Gate" by V. Raymond Edman, quoted by C. Leslie Miller in *All About Angels* (Regal Books, Ventura, CA, © 1973). Used by permission of Dr. C. Leslie Miller.

"As Tall as Trees" by Marilynn Carlson Webber and William D. Webber from *A Rustle of Angels* (Zondervan Publishing House, Grand Rapids, MI, © 1994). Used by permission of Zondervan Publishing House.

"A Prisoner…and Yet" by Corrie ten Boom from *A Prisoner and Yet…* (The Christian Literature Crusade, London, UK and Fort Washington, PA, © 1954). Used by permission.

"Two Came for Katherine" by Gary Kinnaman from *Angels: Dark and Light* (Servant Publications, Box 8617, Ann Arbor, MI 48107, © 1994). Used by permission.

MIRACLES FOR EVERYDAY LIFE

"Incredible" by David Jeremiah from *The Power of Encouragement* (Multnomah Publishers, Inc, Sisters, OR, © 1994).

"A Shield of Protection" by Pat Robertson with William Proctor from *Beyond Reason: How Miracles Can Change Your Life* (William Morrow and Company, Inc, New York, NY, © 1985).

"Don't *Ever* Let Your Guard Down" by Donald Jacobson. Reprinted by permission of *Guideposts Magazine* (Guideposts, Carmel, NY, © 1983).

"Please Lord, Let Her Live" by Kenneth N. Taylor from *My Life: A*

MIRACLES OF PRAYER

MIRACLES OF HEALING

"A Hand on Her Shoulder" by Andrea Gross, "I Met an Angel" in *Ladies Home Journal*, December 1992. Used by permission.

"Beautiful Eyes" by Adrian Rogers from *Believe in Miracles but Trust in Jesus* (Good News Publishers, Crossway Books, Wheaton, IL, © 1997), p. 22. Used by permission. Note: A portion of this excerpt was quoted from *These Blind Eyes Now See* by Marolyn Ford with Phyllis Boykin (Chariot Victor Books, Wheaton, IL, © 1977).

"Getting Straightened Out" by Tony Campolo. Reprinted by permission of the author. All rights reserved.

"Our Daughter's Cancer" by Henry T. Blackaby and Claude King from *Experiencing God* (Broadman and Holman Publishers, Nashville, TN, © 1994). Used by permission. All rights reserved.

"Buried Alive!" by Beth Mullally. This article appeared in the March 1996 edition of the Reader's Digest. Used by permission of the author who lives in Goshen, NY and the Reader's Digest Association, Inc. All rights retained.

"Miracle in My Family" by Dale Hanson Bourke. This article was taken from *Decision* magazine, October 1996, © 1996 Billy Graham Evangelistic Association. Used by permission. All rights reserved.

"The House Church in China" by Carl Lawrence from *The Coming Influence of China* (Multnomah Publishers, Inc, Sisters, OR, © 1996).

MIRACLES OF CHANGED LIVES

"We Were in Row Twenty-six" by Dr. John Aker from *God, You, and That Man with Three Goats* by Dan and Vera Hillis, © 1995. Used by permission of Dr. and Mrs. Don Hillis, 3307 Thurman Ave., Roanoke, VA 24012. All rights retained.

"Jesus...and Jim" by J. Sidlow Baxter from *Awake My Heart* (Zondervan Publishing House, Grand Rapids, MI, © 1960).

"Project Pearl" by Jeff Taylor, from *Artist's Alliance Follow-up Program*, script one. Compass Direct/Open Doors, Santa Ana, CA. Used by permission. All rights retained.

"Uncle Roger" by Rebecca Manley Pippert from *Hope Has Its Reasons* (HarperCollins Publishers, Inc, New York, NY, © 1989 by Rebecca Manley Pippert). Used by permission of HarperCollins Publishers, Inc.

"Let's Sing It!" by Charles Colson from *Kingdoms in Conflict* (William Morrow & Company, Inc, New York, NY, © 1987 by Charles Colson). Used by permission of William Morrow & Company, Inc.

"A Place of Peace" by Jeff Taylor, from *Artist's Alliance Follow-up Program*, script four. Compass Direct/Open Doors, Santa Ana, CA. Used by permission. All rights retained.

THE TWO GREATEST MIRACLES

"God Came" by Joni Eareckson Tada from *A Christmas Longing* (Multnomah Publishers, Inc, Sisters, OR, © 1990, 1996).

"Extraordinary Moment" by Max Lucado from *The Final Week of Jesus* (Multnomah Publishers, Inc, Sisters, OR, © 1994).